"These nineteenth- and early-twentieth-century biographies, now republished by Chelsea House, reveal an unsuspected significance. Not only are a good many of them substantively valuable (and by no means entirely superseded), but they also evoke a sense of the period, an intimacy with the attitudes and assumptions of their times."
—Professor Daniel Aaron

Washington Irving

Other titles in this Chelsea House series:

WASHINGTON IRVING
CHARLES DUDLEY WARNER

INTRODUCTION BY
PHILIP McFARLAND

American Men and Women of Letters Series

GENERAL EDITOR
PROFESSOR DANIEL AARON
HARVARD UNIVERSITY

CHELSEA HOUSE
NEW YORK, LONDON
1980

Copyright © 1980 by Chelsea House Publishers, a division of
Chelsea House Educational Communications, Inc.
All rights reserved
Printed and bound in the United States of America

Library of Congress Cataloging in Publication Data

Warner, Charles Dudley, 1829-1900.
    Washington Irving.

    (American men and women of letters)
    Reprint of the 1884 ed. published by Houghton
Mifflin, Boston, in series: American men of letters.
1. Irving, Washington, 1783-1859.   2. Authors,
American--19th century--Biography.   I. Series.
II. Series: American men of letters.
PS2081.W25 1980   818'.209 [B]   80-23548
ISBN 0-87754-153-1

Chelsea House Publishers
Harold Steinberg, Chairman & Publisher
Andrew E. Norman, President
Susan Lusk, Vice President
A Division of Chelsea House Educational Communications, Inc.
133 Christopher Street, New York 10014

CONTENTS

CHAPTER VIII.

CHAPTER IX.

CHAPTER X.

General Introduction

THE VISITABLE PAST
Daniel Aaron

THE TWENTY-FIVE BIOGRAPHIES of American worthies reissued in this Chelsea House series restore an all but forgotten chapter in the annals of American literary culture. Some of the authors of these volumes—journalists, scholars, writers, professional men—would be considered amateurs by today's standards, but they enjoyed certain advantages not open to their modern counterparts. In some cases they were blood relations or old friends of the men and women they wrote about, or at least near enough to them in time to catch the contemporary essence often missing in the more carefully researched and authoritative later studies of the same figures. Their leisurely, impressionistic accounts—sometimes as interesting for what is omitted as for what is emphasized—reveal a good deal about late Victorian assumptions, cultural and social, and about the vicissitudes of literary reputation.

Each volume in the series is introduced by a recognized scholar who was encouraged to write an idiosyncratic appraisal of the biographer and his work. The introductions vary in emphasis and point of view, for the biographies are not of equal quality, nor are the writers memorialized equally appealing. Yet a kind of consensus is discernible in these random assessments: surprise at the insights still to be found in ostensibly unscientific and old-fashioned works; in some instances admiration for the solidity and liveliness of the biographer's prose and quality of mind; respect for the pioneer historians among them who made excellent use of the limited material at their disposal.

The volumes in this American Men and Women of Letters series contain none of the startling "private" and "personal" episodes modern readers have come to expect in biography, but they illuminate what Henry James called the "visitable past." As such, they are of particular value to all students of American cultural and intellectual history.

Cambridge, Massachusetts
Spring, 1980

INTRODUCTION
TO THE
CHELSEA HOUSE EDITION

Philip McFarland

A century has passed since Charles Dudley Warner's biography of Washington Irving was first published, in 1881. Irving himself had been dead for two decades and more when it appeared, so that the biographer stood in chronological relationship to his subject much as we stand in relation to Ernest Hemingway. Irving and Hemingway: the names look odd in juxtaposition. Yet as different as are, say, *The Sketch Book* and *The Sun Also Rises* in tone, style, form, and subject matter, the authors of those two representative, contrasting works do share some traits. Both Hemingway and Irving were lionized during their life-

times, perhaps extravagantly. In the
early 1820s, with the long Napoleonic
conflict ended, Washington Irving was
pointed out to tourists as he lolled about
postwar Paris; a hundred years later,
after another war, that other expatriate
Hemingway endured the same worship-
ful attention in cafés of the same city.
Both writers gained international fame.
Both exerted a strong influence on their
successors. And twenty years after their
deaths—Irving's just before 1860 (on
November 28, 1859), Hemingway's soon
after 1960 (on July 2, 1961)—the reputation of both writers was in decline.

Warner's account begins with a chapter that sensibly considers the shifting
states of his subject's reputation, what it
had been and what by the early eighties
it had become. "For fifty years," the
biographer writes, "Irving charmed and
instructed the American people, and was
the author who held, on the whole, the
first place in their affections." The asser-
tion is altogether accurate. It is arguable
that no American author before or since

has, during his lifetime, been so highly regarded by so many cultivated readers as was the creator of "Rip Van Winkle" and "The Legend of Sleepy Hollow"—storyteller, essayist, historian, biographer himself, first American to win international fame by his pen alone. Opinions of illustrious contemporaries are indicative. Lord Byron testified that Irving's writings were his delight. Witnesses as different as Scott, Thackeray, Poe, and Hawthorne set down their high regard for this modest, inspiring colleague. Young Charles Dickens wrote Irving, "There is no living writer, and there are very few among the dead, whose approbation I should feel so proud to earn. And with everything you have written upon my shelves, and in my thoughts, and in my heart of hearts, I may honestly and truly say so. . . ."

A chief virtue of the following pages lies in the economy with which they recount an achievement that earned such encomiums from those and so many other distinguished contemporaries, and from thousands and tens of thousands less distinguished though equally enthusiastic readers during Irving's lifetime. We are at some remove from that achievement; but more than a century after Irving's death, two centuries after his birth in 1783, we can here reacquaint ourselves with his wide-ranging life, as well as with the variety and quality of his accomplishment, through the clear, agreeable prose of one who was close in time and spirit to the subject he portrayed.

Charles Dudley Warner had already established his own considerable reputation (though time has proved it perishable) when he wrote his biography of Irving as the initial volume in a projected series on American Men of Letters, which he had agreed to edit. Warner was entering his fifties by then, established as editor of the *Hartford Courant* and author of such lucrative travel books and collections of nostalgic sketches as *Backlog Studies* and *In the Levant.* For the preceding twenty years, since 1860, he had been living in Hartford, member in excellent standing of the Nook Farm circle, which included most notably Harriet Beecher Stowe and Mark Twain. Indeed, it is as collaborator with Mark Twain on *The Gilded Age* (1873) that Warner is best remembered now, though to his disparagement: what strength and humor are found in that satire came from his Missouri friend; the enfeebling sentiment, as is invariably noted, was Warner's contribution.

For our taste sentiment weakens Warner's other imaginative efforts as well, although his evocation of childhood on a New England farm in *Being a Boy* offers a precision of detail that remains engaging. He was born in Plainfield, in western Massachusetts, in 1829. His father, tiller of rocky acres, died when Charles was five; his mother removed with her family to nearby Charlemont, where the boy lived for several years with a guardian and relatives. Yet no such losses and dislocations are allowed to darken the pages of his recollections of childhood days. Instead, the mature Warner chose to remember only such bright details of farm life as driving the oxen to the cider mill with a load of apples, lunching on baked beans and doughnuts and root beer under a tree by a spring, reading by tallow candle near a blazing fire after the evening chores, before being sent too soon to bed.

He was fortunate as a farm boy to have access to books. The works of Irving he read early. Like Irving, who died when the younger writer was thirty, Warner as a youth studied law—had even gone west to Chicago to practice it—but willingly forsook that profession when a friend summoned him back east in 1860 to serve as editor of a recently founded newspaper. His journalistic gifts proved formidable; for the rest of his long life he was associated with what was to become the *Hartford Courant,* first and most actively as its editor, his fluent pen furnishing countless leaders, editorials, and feature sketches. *My Summer in a*

Garden (1871), a collection of humorous sketches on dilettante farming, enjoyed an enormous vogue—its genial manner was compared with Irving's—and made its author famous nationally. That work Warner followed with books of travel on Nova Scotia, California, Europe, and the Near East, none with anything like the lasting appeal of his neighbor's *Innocents Abroad* and *Roughing It,* but all popular enough in their time. And still they provide, with the three satirical, moralizing novels of Warner's later years, ready access to the feelings and interests of post-Civil War America. Busy almost to the last with writing and editorial projects, preoccupied in his old age with the cause of prison reform, Warner died in Hartford in the autumn of 1900, in his seventy-second year, at the start of the new century.

Sentiment, which makes murky what should be clear, often invades Warner's imaginative prose. But the prose in which he casts his life of Irving is ad-

mirably free of murkiness—affectionate
and appreciative, but rarely sentimental.
The account has other merits besides
clarity and conciseness. Despite the century that has passed since its composition it remains for the most part accurate. More is known now, to be sure,
than Warner could know about the relationship in Dresden between the forty-
year-old Irving and the lovely nineteen-
year-old Englishwoman Emily Foster.
The publication in 1938 of Emily's
Dresden journal revealed that more
stood in the way of that complex relationship than Warner thought. Indeed, to
satisfy our curious century, Irving's in-
volvement with women throughout his
life has been considered in detail in
George Hellman's *Washington Irving
Esquire* (1925) and, more authoritative-
ly, in the great two-volume *Life of Washington Irving* by Stanley T. Williams
(1935). But as an introductory account,
Warner's handling of the subject is altogether adequate—and more clear-sighted,
by the way, than the account offered in

the sentimental pages of his predecessor, Irving's own nephew, collaborator, executor, and biographer, Pierre M. Irving, whose four-volume life of his illustrious uncle had appeared in the 1860s.

Whatever inaccuracies occur elsewhere in Warner's book—Colbourne for Cockburn, the painter Leslie where the bookseller Miller should be—these are rare and minor enough, and more than offset by the book's remaining strengths. Foremost is Warner's anecdotal and conversational style. The tone is not unlike Irving's own, demonstrating the affinity between biographer and subject. For example, the publisher Murray's pompous and ill-judged rejection of the manuscript of *The Sketch Book,* Warner slyly notes, was "written in that charming phraseology with which authors are familiar, but which they would in vain seek to imitate." Concerning a friend's charge to Irving that the acerb critic Jeffrey, on a visit to America, must be shown Niagara, Warner remarks, "The impression seems to have prevailed that

if Englishmen could be made to take a
just view of the Falls of Niagara the misunderstandings between the two countries would be reduced." Of Irving's vast
popularity: "His readers were the million, and all his readers were admirers.
Even American statesmen, who feed
their minds on food we know not of,
read Irving." And of his writings: "He
was," says Warner, to whom the same
applies, "always a little in the past
tense."

The pleasure of encountering such
felicities in the matrix of Warner's account is augmented by the extensive
selections provided from Irving's own
prose. Some of that prose is in the form
of letters—letters sometimes "longer and
more elaborate and formal," says Warner, "than this generation has leisure to
write or to read." But the biographer
has extracted from them judiciously, so
that his account of Irving's career is supported at every stage by the voice we
would most want to hear—that of the
subject himself. And though Warner's

book is brief, it has the further advantage of making room in its penultimate
chapter for a generous sampling of
Irving's prose from the range of his published work. With the letters, these extracts provide a good initial representation of the style and tone of a craftsman
whose influence was once so extensive,
whose grace and charm can still give
abundant delight, and whose lasting significance Warner himself astutely judges
in conclusion.

An additional merit of the study
might be mentioned, an accidental merit
but one that provides its own satisfac-
tions. We in the 1980s read a book written in the 1880s about a writer born in
the 1780s. Movement among the three
centuries allows for recognitions and
ironies. We learn, for instance, with a-
mused sympathy that as far back in the
past as a hundred years ago, "the attention of young and old readers has been
so occupied and distracted by the flood
of new books, written with the single
purpose of satisfying the wants of the

day, . . . that the standard works of approved literature remain for the most part unread upon the shelves." Again, of the abolitionist cause, we are told that "to 'lift up the voice' and wear long hair were signs of devotion to a purpose." Yet again, the delicious humor of *Knickerbocker's History* "occasionally has a breadth that is indelicate to our apprehension," so the biographer feels, "though it perhaps did not shock our great-grandmothers."

Nor would it his great-grandchildren. Such effects of perspective might in themselves be reason for preferring Warner's book—concise as it is, and accurate in the main—over all others as an introduction to the diffident author whose achievement may after all justify that title the textbooks long ago assigned him: Father of American Literature.

Lexington, Massachusetts
July, 1980

WASHINGTON IRVING

WASHINGTON IRVING.

CHAPTER I.

PRELIMINARY.

IT is over twenty years since the death of Washington Irving removed that personal presence which is always a powerful, and sometimes the sole, stimulus to the sale of an author's books, and which strongly affects the contemporary judgment of their merits. It is nearly a century since his birth, which was almost coeval with that of the Republic, for it took place the year the British troops evacuated the city of New York, and only a few months before General Washington marched in at the head of the Continental army and took possession of the metropolis. For fifty years Irving charmed and instructed the American people, and was the author who held, on the whole, the first place in their affections. As he was

1

the first to lift American literature into the popular respect of Europe, so for a long time he was the chief representative of the American name in the world of letters. During this period probably no citizen of the Republic, except the Father of his Country, had so wide a reputation as his namesake, Washington Irving.

It is time to inquire what basis this great reputation had in enduring qualities, what portion of it was due to local and favoring circumstances, and to make an impartial study of the author's literary rank and achievement.

The tenure of a literary reputation is the most uncertain and fluctuating of all. The popularity of an author seems to depend quite as much upon fashion or whim, as upon a change in taste or in literary form. Not only is contemporary judgment often at fault, but posterity is perpetually revising its opinion. We are accustomed to say that the final rank of an author is settled by the slow consensus of mankind in disregard of the critics; but the rank is after all determined by the few best minds of any given age, and the popular judgment has

very little to do with it. Immediate popularity, or currency, is a nearly valueless cri-
terion of merit. The settling of high rank
even in the popular mind does not necessarily give currency; the so-called best
authors are not those most widely read at
any given time. Some who attain the
position of classics are subject to variations
in popular and even in scholarly favor or
neglect. It happens to the princes of literature to encounter periods of varying dura-
tion when their names are revered and their
books are not read. The growth, not to
say the fluctuation, of Shakespeare's popularity is one of the curiosities of literary
history. Worshiped by his contemporaries,
apostrophized by Milton only fourteen years
after his death as the " dear son of memory,
great heir to fame," —

> " So sepulchred in such pomp dost lie,
> That kings, for such a tomb, would wish to die," —

he was neglected by the succeeding age,
the subject of violent extremes of opinion
in the eighteenth century, and so lightly esteemed by some that Hume could doubt if
he were a poet " capable of furnishing a
proper entertainment to a refined and in-

telligent audience," and attribute to the rudeness of his "disproportioned and mis-shapen" genius the "reproach of bar-barism" which the English nation had suffered from all its neighbors. Only recently has the study of him by English scholars — I do not refer to the verbal squabbles over the text — been proportioned to his preëminence, and his fame is still slowly asserting itself among foreign peoples.

There are already signs that we are not to accept as the final judgment upon the English contemporaries of Irving the currency their writings have now. In the case of Walter Scott, although there is already visible a reaction against a reaction, he is not, at least in America, read by this generation as he was by the last. This faint reaction is no doubt a sign of a deeper change impending in philosophic and metaphysical speculation. An age is apt to take a lurch in a body one way or another, and those most active in it do not always perceive how largely its direction is determined by what are called mere systems of philosophy. The novelist may not know whether he is steered by Kant, or Hegel, or Schopenhauer. The humanitarian novel, the fictions of passion, of realism, of doubt, the poetry and the essays addressed to the mood of unrest, of questioning, to the scientific spirit and to the shifting attitudes of social change and reform, claim the attention of an age that is completely adrift in regard to the relations of the supernatural and the material, the ideal and the real. It would be natural if in such a time of confusion the calm tones of unexaggerated literary art should be not so much heeded as the more strident voices. Yet when the passing fashion of this day is succeeded by the fashion of another, that which is most acceptable to the thought and feeling of the present may be without an audience ; and it may happen that few recent authors will be read as Scott and the writers of the early part of this century will be read. It may, however, be safely predicted that those writers of fiction worthy to be called literary artists will best retain their hold who have faithfully painted the manners of their own time.

Irving has shared the neglect of the writers of his generation. It would be strange, even in America, if this were not so. The development of American literature (using the term in its broadest sense) in the past forty years is greater than could have been expected in a nation which had its ground to clear, its wealth to win, and its new governmental experiment to adjust; if we confine our view to the last twenty years, the national production is vast in amount and encouraging in quality. It suffices to say of it here, in a general way, that the most vigorous activity has been in the departments of history, of applied science, and the discussion of social and economic problems. Although pure literature has made considerable gains, the main achievement has been in other directions. The audience of the literary artist has been less than that of the reporter of affairs and discoveries and the special correspondent. The age is too busy, too harassed, to have time for literature; and enjoyment of writings like those of Irving depends upon leisure of mind. The mass of readers have cared less for form than for novelty and news and the satisfying of a recently awakened curiosity.

This was inevitable in an era of journalism, one marked by the marvelous results attained in the fields of religion, science, and art, by the adoption of the comparative method. Perhaps there is no better illustration of the vigor and intellectual activity of the age than a living English writer, who has traversed and illuminated almost every province of modern thought, controversy, and scholarship; but who supposes that Mr. Gladstone has added anything to permanent literature? He has been an immense force in his own time, and his influence the next generation will still feel and acknowledge, while it reads not the writings of Mr. Gladstone but may be those of the author of "Henry Esmond" and the biographer of "Rab and his Friends." De Quincey divides literature into two sorts, the literature of power and the literature of knowledge. The latter is of necessity for to-day only, and must be revised to-morrow. The definition has scarcely De Quincey's usual verbal felicity, but we can apprehend the distinction he intended to make.

It is to be noted also, and not with regard to Irving only, that the attention of

young and old readers has been so occupied
and distracted by the flood of new books,
written with the single purpose of satisfying the wants of the day, produced and distributed with marvelous cheapness and facility, that the standard works of approved
literature remain for the most part unread
upon the shelves. Thirty years ago Irving
was much read in America by young people, and his clear style helped to form a
good taste and correct literary habits. It
is not so now. The manufacturers of books,
periodicals, and newspapers for the young
keep the rising generation fully occupied,
with a result to its taste and mental fibre
which, to say the least of it, must be
regarded with some apprehension. The
"plant," in the way of money and writing
industry invested in the production of juvenile literature, is so large and is so permanent an interest, that it requires more discriminating consideration than can be given
to it in a passing paragraph.

Besides this, and with respect to Irving
in particular, there has been in America a
criticism — sometimes called the destruc-
tive, sometimes the Donnybrook Fair —

that found "earnestness" the only thing in the world amusing, that brought to literary art the test of utility, and disparaged what is called the "Knickerbocker School" (assuming Irving to be the head of it) as wanting in purpose and virility, a merely romantic development of the post-Revolutionary period. And it has been to some extent the fashion to damn with faint admiration the pioneer if not the creator of American literature as the "genial" Irving.

Before I pass to an outline of the career of this representative American author, it is necessary to refer for a moment to certain periods, more or less marked, in our literature. I do not include in it the works of writers either born in England or completely English in training, method, and tradition, showing nothing distinctively American in their writings except the incidental subject. The first authors whom we may regard as characteristic of the new country — leaving out the productions of speculative theology — devoted their genius to politics. It is in the political writings immediately preceding and following the Revolution— such as those of Hamilton, Madison,

Jay, Franklin, Jefferson — that the new
birth of a nation of original force and ideas
is declared. It has been said, and I think
the statement can be maintained, that for
any parallel to those treatises on the nature
of government, in respect to originality and
vigor, we must go back to classic times.
But literature, that is, literature which is
an end in itself and not a means to something else, did not exist in America before Irving. Some foreshadowings (the au-
tobiographical fragment of Franklin was
not published till 1817) of its coming may
be traced, but there can be no question that
his writings were the first that bore the
national literary stamp, that he first made
the nation conscious of its gift and opportunity, and that he first announced to
trans-Atlantic readers the entrance of America upon the literary field. For some time
he was our only man of letters who had a
reputation beyond seas.

Irving was not, however, the first American who made literature a profession and
attempted to live on its fruits. This distinction belongs to Charles Brockden Brown,
who was born in Philadelphia, January 17,

1771, and, before the appearance in a newspaper of Irving's juvenile essays in 1802,
had published several romances, which were
hailed as original and striking productions
by his contemporaries, and even attracted
attention in England. As late as 1820 a
prominent British review gives Mr. Brown
the first rank in our literature as an original writer and characteristically American.
The reader of to-day who has the curiosity
to inquire into the correctness of this opinion will, if he is familiar with the romances
of the eighteenth century, find little originality in Brown's stories, and nothing distinctively American. The figures who are
moved in them seem to be transported from
the pages of foreign fiction to the New
World, not as it was, but as it existed in
the minds of European sentimentalists.

Mr. Brown received a fair education in a
classical school in his native city, and studied
law, which he abandoned on the threshold
of practice, as Irving did, and for the same
reason. He had the genuine literary impulse, which he obeyed against all the ar-
guments and entreaties of his friends. Unfortunately, with a delicate physical consti-

tution he had a mind of romantic sensibility, and in the comparative inaction imposed
by his frail health he indulged in vision-
ary speculation, and in solitary wanderings
which developed the habit of sentimental
musing. It was natural that such reveries
should produce morbid romances. The
tone of them is that of the unwholesome
fiction of his time, in which the "seducer"
is a prominent and recognized character in
social life, and female virtue is the frail
sport of opportunity. Brown's own life
was fastidiously correct, but it is a curious
commentary upon his estimate of the natural power of resistance to vice in his time,
that he regarded his feeble health as good
fortune, since it protected him from the
temptations of youth and virility.

While he was reading law he constantly
exercised his pen in the composition of essays, some of which were published under
the title of the " Rhapsodist ; " but it was
not until 1797 that his career as an author
began, by the publication of "Alcuin : a Dia-
logue on the Rights of Women." This and
the romances which followed it show the
powerful influence upon him of the school of

fiction of William Godwin, and the movement of emancipation of which Mary Woll-
stonecraft was the leader. The period of
social and political ferment during which
" Alcuin " was put forth was not unlike that
which may be said to have reached its
height in extravagance and millennial expectation in 1847–48. In " Alcuin " are anticipated most of the subsequent discussions on
the right of women to property and to self-
control, and the desirability of revising the
marriage relation. The injustice of any more
enduring union than that founded upon the
inclination of the hour is as ingeniously
urged in " Alcuin " as it has been in our own
day.

Mr. Brown's reputation rests upon six
romances : " Wieland," " Ormond," " Arthur Mervyn," " Edgar Huntly," " Clara
Howard," and " Jane Talbot." The first five
were published in the interval between the
spring of 1798 and the summer of 1801, in
which he completed his thirtieth year.
" Jane Talbot " appeared somewhat later.
In scenery and character, these romances
are entirely unreal. There is in them an
affectation of psychological purpose which

is not very well sustained, and a somewhat
clumsy introduction of supernatural machin-
ery. Yet they have a power of engaging
the attention in the rapid succession of startling and uncanny incidents and in adventures in which the horrible is sometimes
dangerously near the ludicrous. Brown had
not a particle of humor. Of literary art
there is little, of invention considerable;
and while the style is to a certain extent
unformed and immature, it is neither feeble
nor obscure, and admirably serves the author's purpose of creating what the children
call a "crawly" impression. There is un-
deniable power in many of his scenes, notably in the descriptions of the yellow fever
in Philadelphia, found in the romance of
"Arthur Mervyn." There is, however,
over all of them a false and pallid light; his
characters are seen in a spectral atmosphere.
If a romance is to be judged not by literary
rules, but by its power of making an impression upon the mind, such power as a
ghastly story has, told by the chimney-
corner on a tempestuous night, then Mr.
Brown's romances cannot be dismissed without a certain recognition. But they never

represented anything distinctively American, and their influence upon American literature is scarcely discernible.

Subsequently Mr. Brown became interested in political subjects, and wrote upon them with vigor and sagacity. He was the editor of two short-lived literary periodicals which were nevertheless useful in their day: "The Monthly Magazine and American Review," begun in New York in the spring of 1798, and ending in the autumn of 1800; and "The Literary Magazine and American Register," which was established in Philadelphia in 1803. It was for this periodical that Mr. Brown, who visited Irving in that year, sought in vain to enlist the service of the latter, who, then a youth of nineteen, had a little reputation as the author of some humorous essays in the "Morning Chronicle" newspaper.

Charles Brockden Brown died, the victim of a lingering consumption, in 1810, at the age of thirty-nine. In pausing for a moment upon his incomplete and promising career, we should not forget to recall the strong impression he made upon his contemporaries as a man of genius, the testimony to the charm of his conversation and the goodness of his heart, nor the pioneer service he rendered to letters before the provincial fetters were at all loosened.

The advent of Cooper, Bryant, and Halleck, was some twenty years after the recognition of Irving, but thereafter the stars thicken in our literary sky, and when in 1832 Irving returned from his long sojourn in Europe, he found an immense advance in fiction, poetry, and historical composition. American literature was not only born, — it was able to go alone. We are not likely to overestimate the stimulus to this movement given by Irving's example, and by his success abroad. His leadership is recognized in the respectful attitude towards him of all his contemporaries in America. And the cordiality with which he gave help whenever it was asked, and his eagerness to acknowledge merit in others, secured him the affection of all the literary class, which is popularly supposed to have a rare appreciation of the defects of fellow craftsmen.

The period from 1830 to 1860 was that of our greatest purely literary achievement, and, indeed, most of the greater names of to-day were familiar before 1850. Conspicuous exceptions are Motley and Parkman and a few belles-lettres writers, whose novels and stories mark a distinct literary transition since the War of the Rebellion. In the period from 1845 to 1860, there was a singular development of sentimentalism; it had been growing before, it did not altogether disappear at the time named, and it was so conspicuous that this may properly be called the sentimental era in our literature. The causes of it, and its relation to our changing national character, are worthy the study of the historian. In politics, the discussion of constitutional questions, of tariffs and finance, had given way to moral agitations. Every political movement was determined by its relation. to slavery. Eccentricities of all sorts were developed. It was the era of "transcendentalism" in New England, of "come-outers" there and elsewhere, of communistic experiments; of reform notions about marriage, about woman's dress, about diet; through the open door of abolitionism women appeared upon its platform, demanding a various emancipation; the agitation for total abstinence from intoxicating drinks got under full headway, urged on moral rather than on the statistical and scientific grounds of to-day; reformed drunkards went about from town to town depicting to applauding audiences the horrors of delirium tremens, — one of these peripatetics led about with him a goat, perhaps as a scapegoat and sin-offering; tobacco was as odious as rum; and I remember that George Thompson, the eloquent apostle of emancipation, during his tour in this country, when on one occasion he was the cynosure of a protracted antislavery meeting at Peterboro, the home of Gerrit Smith, deeply offended some of his coworkers, and lost the admiration of many of his admirers, the maiden devotees of green tea, by his use of snuff. To "lift up the voice" and wear long hair were signs of devotion to a purpose.

In that seething time, the lighter literature took a sentimental tone, and either spread itself in manufactured fine writing, or lapsed into a reminiscent and melting mood. In a pretty affectation, we were asked to meditate upon the old garret, the deserted hearth, the old letters, the old well-sweep, the dead baby, the little shoes ; we were put into a mood in which we were defenseless against the lukewarm flood of the Tupperean Philosophy. Even the newspapers caught the bathetic tone. Every "local" editor breathed his woe over the incidents of the police court, the falling leaf, the tragedies of the boarding-house, in the most lachrymose periods he could command, and let us never lack fine writing, whatever might be the dearth of news. I need not say how suddenly and completely this affectation was laughed out of sight by the coming of the "humorous" writer, whose existence is justified by the excellent service he performed in clearing the tearful atmosphere. His keen and mocking method, which is quite distinct from the humor of Goldsmith and Irving, and differs, in degree at least, from the comic almanac exaggeration and coarseness which preceded it, puts its foot on every bud of sentiment, holds few things sacred, and refuses to regard anything in life seriously. But it has no mercy for any sham.

I refer to this sentimental era — remembering that its literary manifestation was only a surface disease, and recognizing fully the value of the great moral movement in purifying the national life — because many regard its literary weakness as a legitimate outgrowth of the Knickerbocker School, and hold Irving in a manner responsible for it. But I find nothing in the manly sentiment and true tenderness of Irving to warrant the sentimental gush of his followers, who missed his corrective humor as completely as they failed to catch his literary art. Whatever note of localism there was in the Knickerbocker School, however *dilettante* and unfruitful it was, it was not the legitimate heir of the broad and eclectic genius of Irving. The nature of that genius we shall see in his life.

CHAPTER II.

BOYHOOD.

WASHINGTON IRVING was born in the city of New York, April 3, 1783. He was the eighth son of William and Sarah Irving, and the youngest of eleven children, three of whom died in infancy. His parents, though of good origin, began life in humble circumstances. His father was born on the island of Shapinska. His family, one of the most respectable in Scotland, traced its descent from William De Irwyn, the secretary and armor-bearer of Robert Bruce; but at the time of the birth of William Irving its fortunes had gradually decayed, and the lad sought his livelihood, according to the habit of the adventurous Orkney Islanders, on the sea.

It was during the French War, and while he was serving as a petty officer in an armed packet plying between Falmouth and New York, that he met Sarah Sanders, a

beautiful girl, the only daughter of John
and Anna Sanders, who had the distinction
of being the granddaughter of an English
curate.   The youthful pair were married in
1761, and two years after embarked for
New York, where they landed July 18,
1763.   Upon settling in New York William Irving quit the sea and took to trade,
in which he was successful until his business was broken up by the Revolutionary
War.   In this contest he was a staunch
Whig, and suffered for his opinions at the
hands of the British occupants of the city,
and both he and his wife did much to alle-
viate the misery of the American prisoners.
In this charitable ministry his wife, who
possessed a rarely generous and sympathetic
nature, was especially zealous, supplying
the prisoners with food from her own table,
visiting those who were ill, and furnishing
them with clothing and other necessaries.

Washington was born in a house on William Street, about half-way between Fulton
and John; the following year the family
moved across the way into one of the quaint
structures of the time, its gable end with
attic window towards the street, the fash-

ion of which, and very likely the bricks, came from Holland. In this homestead the lad grew up, and it was not pulled down till 1849, ten years before his death. The patriot army occupied the city. "Washington's work is ended," said the mother, "and the child shall be named after him." When the first President was again in New York, the first seat of the new government, a Scotch maid-servant of the family, catching the popular enthusiasm, one day followed the hero into a shop and presented the lad to him. "Please, your honor," said Lizzie, all aglow, "here's a bairn was named after you." And the grave Virginian placed his hand on the boy's head and gave him his blessing. The touch could not have been more efficacious, though it might have lingered longer, if he had known he was propitiating his future biographer.

New York at the time of our author's birth was a rural city of about twenty-three thousand inhabitants, clustered about the Battery. It did not extend northward to the site of the present City Hall Park; and beyond, then and for several years afterwards, were only country residences, or-

chards, and corn-fields. The city was half
burned down during the war, and had
emerged from it in a dilapidated condition.
There was still a marked separation between
the Dutch and the English residents, though
the Irvings seem to have been on terms of
intimacy with the best of both nationalities.
The habits of living were primitive ; the
manners were agreeably free ; conviviality
at the table was the fashion, and strong ex-
pletives had not gone out of use in conversation. Society was the reverse of intellectual : the aristocracy were the merchants
and traders ; what literary culture found
expression was formed on English models,
dignified and plentifully garnished with
Latin and Greek allusions; the commercial
spirit ruled, and the relaxations and amusements partook of its hurry and excitement.
In their gay, hospitable, and mercurial character, the inhabitants were true progenitors
of the present metropolis. A newspaper
had been established in 1732, and a theatre
had existed since 1750. Although the town
had a rural aspect, with its quaint dormer-
window houses, its straggling lanes and
roads, and the water-pumps in the middle

of the streets, it had the aspirations of a city, and already much of the metropolitan air.

These were the surroundings in which the boy's literary talent was to develop. His father was a deacon in the Presbyterian church, a sedate, God-fearing man, with the strict severity of the Scotch Covenanter, serious in his intercourse with his family, without sympathy in the amusements of his children; he was not without tenderness in his nature, but the exhibition of it was repressed on principle, — a man of high character and probity, greatly esteemed by his associates. He endeavored to bring up his children in sound religious principles, and to leave no room in their lives for triviality. One of the two weekly half-holidays was required for the catechism, and the only relaxation from the three church services on Sunday was the reading of " Pilgrim's Progress." This cold and severe discipline at home would have been intolerable but for the more lovingly demonstrative and impulsive character of the mother, whose gentle nature and fine intellect won the tender veneration of her children. Of the father

they stood in awe; his conscientious piety
failed to waken any religious sensibility in
them, and they revolted from a teaching
which seemed to regard everything that
was pleasant as wicked. The mother,
brought up an Episcopalian, conformed to
the religious forms and worship of her husband, but she was never in sympathy with
his rigid views. The children were re-
pelled from the creed of their father, and
subsequently all of them except one became
attached to the Episcopal Church. Washington, in order to make sure of his escape,
and feel safe while he was still constrained
to attend his father's church, went stealth-
ily to Trinity Church at an early age, and
received the rite of confirmation. The boy
was full of vivacity, drollery, and innocent
mischief. His sportiveness and disinclination to religious seriousness gave his mother
some anxiety, and she would look at him,
says his biographer, with a half mournful
admiration, and exclaim, " O Washington!
if you were only good!" He had a love of
music, which became later in life a passion,
and great fondness for the theatre. The
stolen delight of the theatre he first tasted

in company with a boy who was somewhat his senior, but destined to be his literary comrade, — James K. Paulding, whose sister was the wife of Irving's brother William. Whenever he could afford this indulgence, he stole away early to the theatre in John Street, remained until it was time to return to the family prayers at nine, after which he would retire to his room, slip through his window and down the roof to a back alley, and return to enjoy the after-piece.

Young Irving's school education was desultory, pursued under several more or less incompetent masters, and was over at the age of sixteen. The teaching does not seem to have had much discipline or solidity; he studied Latin a few months, but made no other incursion into the classics. The handsome, tender-hearted, truthful, susceptible boy was no doubt a dawdler in routine studies, but he assimilated what suited him. He found his food in such pieces of English literature as were floating about, in " Robinson Crusoe " and " Sinbad ; " at ten he was inspired by a translation of " Orlando Furioso ; " he devoured books of voyages and travel; he could turn a neat verse,

and his scribbling propensities were exercised in the composition of childish plays.
The fact seems to be that the boy was a
dreamer and saunterer; he himself says that
he used to wander about the pier heads in
fine weather, watch the ships departing on
long voyages, and dream of going to the
ends of the earth. His brothers Peter and
John had been sent to Columbia College,
and it is probable that Washington would
have had the same advantage if he had not
shown a disinclination to methodical study.
At the age of sixteen he entered a law office,
but he was a heedless student, and never acquired either a taste for the profession or
much knowledge of law. While he sat in
the law office, he read literature, and made
considerable progress in his self-culture; but
he liked rambling and society quite as well
as books. In 1798 we find him passing a
summer holiday in Westchester County,
and exploring with his gun the Sleepy Hollow region which he was afterwards to make
an enchanted realm; and in 1800 he made
his first voyage up the Hudson, the beauties
of which he was the first to celebrate, on a
visit to a married sister who lived in the

Mohawk Valley. In 1802 he became a law clerk in the office of Josiah Ogden Hoffman, and began that enduring intimacy with the refined and charming Hoffman family which was so deeply to influence all his life. His health had always been delicate, and his friends were now alarmed by symptoms of pulmonary weakness. This physical disability no doubt had much to do with his disinclination to severe study. For the next two or three years much time was consumed in excursions up the Hudson and the Mohawk, and in adventurous journeys as far as the wilds of Ogdensburg and to Montreal, to the great improvement of his physical condition, and in the enjoyment of the gay society of Albany, Schenectady, Ballston, and Saratoga Springs. These explorations and visits gave him material for future use, and exercised his pen in agreeable correspondence; but his tendency at this time, and for several years afterwards, was to the idle life of a man of society. Whether the literary impulse which was born in him would have ever insisted upon any but an occasional and fitful expression, except for the necessities of his subsequent condition, is doubtful.

Irving's first literary publication was a series of letters, signed Jonathan Oldstyle, contributed in 1802 to the " Morning Chronicle," a newspaper then recently established by his brother Peter. The attention that these audacious satires of the theatre, the actors, and their audience attracted is evidence of the literary poverty of the period. The letters are open imitations of the " Spectator " and the " Tatler," and although sharp upon local follies are of no consequence at present except as foreshadowing the sensibility and quiet humor of the future author, and his chivalrous devotion to woman. What is worthy of note is that a boy of nineteen should turn aside from his caustic satire to protest against the cruel and unmanly habit of jesting at ancient maidens. It was enough for him that they are women, and possess the strongest claim upon our admiration, tenderness, and protection.

CHAPTER III.

IRVING'S health, always delicate, continued so much impaired when he came of age, in 1804, that his brothers determined to send him to Europe. On the 19th of May he took passage for Bordeaux in a sailing vessel, which reached the mouth of the Garonne on the 25th of June. His consumptive appearance when he went on board caused the captain to say to himself, "There's a chap who will go overboard before we get across;" but his condition was much improved by the voyage.

He stayed six weeks at Bordeaux to improve himself in the language, and then set out for the Mediterranean. In the diligence he had some merry companions, and the party amused itself on the way. It was their habit to stroll about the towns in which they stopped, and talk with whomever they met. Among his companions was a

young French officer and an eccentric, gar-
rulous doctor from America. At Tonneins,
on the Garonne, they entered a house where
a number of girls were quilting. The girls
gave Irving a needle and set him to work.
He could not understand their patois, and
they could not comprehend his bad French,
and they got on very merrily. At last the
little doctor told them that the interesting
young man was an English prisoner whom
the French officer had in custody. Their
merriment at once gave place to pity.
"Ah! le pauvre garçon!" said one to another; "he is merry, however, in all his
trouble." "And what will they do with
him?" asked a young woman. "Oh, nothing of consequence," replied the doctor;
"perhaps shoot him, or cut off his head."
The good souls were much distressed; they
brought him wine, loaded his pockets with
fruit, and bade him good-by with a hundred
benedictions. Over forty years after, Irving made a detour, on his way from Madrid to Paris, to visit Tonneins, drawn thither
solely by the recollection of this incident,
vaguely hoping perhaps to apologize to the
tender-hearted villagers for the imposition.

His conscience had always pricked him for it; "It was a shame," he said, "to leave them with such painful impressions." The quilting party had dispersed by that time. "I believe I recognized the house," he says; "and I saw two or three old women who might once have formed part of the merry group of girls; but I doubt whether they recognized, in the stout elderly gentleman, thus rattling in his carriage through their streets, the pale young English prisoner of forty years since."

Bonaparte was emperor. The whole country was full of suspicion. The police suspected the traveler, notwithstanding his passport, of being an Englishman and a spy, and dogged him at every step. He arrived at Avignon, full of enthusiasm at the thought of seeing the tomb of Laura. "Judge of my surprise," he writes, "my disappointment, and my indignation, when I was told that the church, tomb, and all were utterly demolished in the time of the Revolution. Never did the Revolution, its authors and its consequences, receive a more hearty and sincere execration than at that moment. Throughout the whole of my

3

journey I had found reason to exclaim against it for depriving me of some valuable curiosity or celebrated monument, but this was the severest disappointment it had yet occasioned." This view of the Revolution is very characteristic of Irving, and perhaps the first that would occur to a man of letters. The journey was altogether disagreeable, even to a traveler used to the rough jaunts in an American wilderness: the inns were miserable; dirt, noise, and insolence reigned without control. But it never was our author's habit to stroke the world the wrong way: " When I cannot get a dinner to suit my taste, I endeavor to get a taste to suit my dinner." And he adds: " There is nothing I dread more than to be taken for one of the Smell-fungi of this world. I therefore endeavor to be pleased with everything about me, and with the masters, mistresses, and servants of the inns, particularly when I perceive they have ' all the dispositions in the world' to serve me; as Sterne says, 'It is enough for heaven and ought to be enough for me.' "

The traveler was detained at Marseilles, and five weeks at Nice, on one frivolous pretext of the police or another, and did not reach Genoa till the 20th of October. At Genoa there was a delightful society, and Irving seems to have been more attracted by that than by the historical curiosities. His health was restored, and his spirits recovered elasticity in the genial hospitality; he was surrounded by friends to whom he became so much attached that it was with pain he parted from them. The gayety of city life, the levees of the Doge, and the balls were not unattractive to the handsome young man; but what made Genoa seem like home to him was his intimacy with a few charming families, among whom he mentions those of Mrs. Bird, Madame Gabriac, and Lady Shaftesbury. From the latter he experienced the most cordial and unreserved friendship; she greatly interested herself in his future, and furnished him with letters from herself and the nobility to persons of the first distinction in Florence, Rome, and Naples.

Late in December Irving sailed for Sicily in a Genoese packet. Off the island of Planoca it was overpowered and captured by a little pickaroon, with lateen sails and a couple of guns, and a most villainous crew, in poverty-stricken garments, rusty cutlasses in their hands and stilettos and pistols stuck in their waistbands. The pirates thoroughly ransacked the vessel, opened all the trunks and portmanteaus, but found little that they wanted except brandy and provisions. In releasing the vessel, the ragamuffins seem to have had a touch of humor, for they gave the captain a "receipt" for what they had taken, and an order on the British consul at Messina to pay for the same. This old-time courtesy was hardly appreciated at the moment.

Irving passed a couple of months in Sicily, exploring with some thoroughness the ruins, and making several perilous inland trips, for the country was infested by banditti. One journey from Syracuse through the centre of the island revealed more wretchedness than Irving supposed existed in the world. The half-starved peasants lived in wretched cabins and often in caverns, amid filth and vermin. "God knows my mind never suffered so much as on this journey," he writes, "when I saw such scenes of want and misery continually before me, without the power of effectually relieving them." His stay in the ports was made agreeable by the officers of American ships cruising in those waters. Every ship was a home, and every officer a friend. He had a boundless capacity for good-fellowship. At Messina he chronicles the brilliant spectacle of Lord Nelson's fleet passing through the straits in search of the French fleet that had lately got out of Toulon. In less than a year, Nelson's young admirer was one of the thousands that pressed to see the remains of the great admiral as they lay in state at Greenwich, wrapped in the flag that had floated at the mast-head of the Victory.

From Sicily he passed over to Naples in a fruit boat which dodged the cruisers, and reached Rome the last of March. Here he remained several weeks, absorbed by the multitudinous attractions. In Italy the worlds of music and painting were for the first time opened to him. Here he made the acquaintance of Washington Allston, and the influence of this friendship came near changing the whole course of his life. To return home to the dry study of the

law was not a pleasing prospect; the masterpieces of art, the serenity of the sky, the
nameless charm which hangs about an
Italian landscape, and Allston's enthusiasm
as an artist, nearly decided him to remain
in Rome and adopt the profession of a
painter. But after indulging in this dream,
it occurred to him that it was not so much
a natural aptitude for the art as the lovely
scenery and Allston's companionship that
had attracted him to it. He saw something
of Roman society; Torlonia the banker
was especially assiduous in his attentions.
It turned out when Irving came to make his
adieus that Torlonia had all along supposed
him a relative of General Washington.
This mistake is offset by another that occurred later, after Irving had attained some
celebrity in England. An English lady
passing through an Italian gallery with her
daughter stopped before a bust of Washington. The daughter said, "Mother, who
was Washington?" "Why, my dear, don't
you know?" was the astonished reply.
" He wrote the ' Sketch-Book.' " It was at
the house of Baron von Humboldt, the Prus-
sian minister, that Irving first met Madame

de Staël, who was then enjoying the celebrity of "Delphine." He was impressed with her strength of mind, and somewhat astounded at the amazing flow of her conversation, and the question upon question with which she plied him.

In May the wanderer was in Paris, and remained there four months, studying French and frequenting the theatres with exemplary regularity. Of his life in Paris there are only the meagrest reports, and he records no observations upon political affairs. The town fascinated him more than any other in Europe; he notes that the city is rapidly beautifying under the emperor, that the people seem gay and happy, and *Vive la bagatelle!* is again the burden of their song. His excuse for remissness in correspondence was, " I am a young man and in Paris."

By way of the Netherlands he reached London in October and remained in England till January. The attraction in London seems to have been the theatre, where he saw John Kemble, Cooke, and Mrs. Siddons. Kemble's acting seemed to him too studied and over-labored; he had the disadvantage

of a voice lacking rich, base tones. Whatever he did was judiciously conceived and
perfectly executed; it satisfied the head,
but rarely touched the heart. Only in the
part of Zanga was the young critic completely overpowered by his acting,—Kemble
seemed to have forgotten himself. Cooke,
who had less range than Kemble, completely satisfied Irving as Iago. Of Mrs.
Siddons, who was then old, he scarcely dares
to give his impressions lest he should be
thought extravagant. "Her looks," he says,
"her voice, her gestures, delighted me. She
penetrated in a moment to my heart. She
froze and melted it by turns ; a glance of
her eye, a start, an exclamation, thrilled
through my whole frame. The more I see
her the more I admire her. I hardly breathe
while she is on the stage. She works up
my feelings till I am like a mere child."
Some years later, after the publication of
the "Sketch-Book," in a London assembly
Irving was presented to the tragedy queen,
who had left the stage, but had not laid
aside its stately manner. She looked at
him a moment, and then in a deep-toned
voice slowly enunciated, " You 've made me

weep." The author was so disconcerted that he said not a word, and retreated in confusion. After the publication of "Brace-bridge Hall" he met her in company again, and was persuaded to go through the ordeal of another presentation. The stately woman fixed her eyes on him as before, and slowly said, "You've made me weep again." This time the bashful author acquitted himself with more honor.

This first sojourn abroad was not immediately fruitful in a literary way, and need not further detain us. It was the irresolute pilgrimage of a man who had not yet received his vocation. Everywhere he was received in the best society, and the charm of his manner and his ingenuous nature made him everywhere a favorite. He carried that indefinable passport which society recognizes and which needs no *visé*. He saw the people who were famous, the women whose recognition is a social reputation; he made many valuable friends; he frequented the theatre, he indulged his passion for the opera; he learned how to dine, and to appreciate the delights of a brilliant salon; he was picking up languages; he was observing nature and men, and especially women. That he profited by his loitering experience is plain enough afterward, but thus far there is little to prophesy that Irving would be anything more in life than a charming *flâneur*.

CHAPTER IV.

SOCIETY AND "SALMAGUNDI."

On Irving's return to America in February, 1806, with reëstablished health, life did not at first take on a more serious purpose. He was admitted to the bar, but he still halted.[1] Society more than ever attracted him and devoured his time. He willingly accepted the office of "champion at the tea-parties;" he was one of a knot of young fellows of literary tastes and convivial habits, who delighted to be known

[1] Irving once illustrated his legal acquirements at this time by the relation of the following anecdote to his nephew: Josiah Ogden Hoffman and Martin Wilkins, an effective and witty advocate, had been appointed to examine students for admission. One student acquitted himself very lamely, and at the supper which it was the custom for the candidates to give to the examiners, when they passed upon their several merits, Hoffman paused in coming to this one, and turning to Wilkins said, as if in hesitation, though all the while intending to admit him, "Martin, I think he knows a *little* law." "Make it stronger, Jo," was the reply; "*d——d little.*"

as " The Nine Worthies," or " Lads of Kil-
kenny." In his letters of this period I de-
tect a kind of callowness and affectation
which is not discernible in his foreign letters
and journal.

These social worthies had jolly suppers
at the humble taverns of the city, and
wilder revelries in an old country house on
the Passaic, which is celebrated in the " Salmagundi " papers as Cockloft Hall. We
are reminded of the change of manners by
a letter of Mr. Paulding, one of his com-
rades, written twenty years after, who recalls to mind the keeper of a porter house,
" who whilom wore a long coat, in the
pockets whereof he jingled two bushels of
sixpenny pieces, and whose daughter played
the piano to the accompaniment of broiled
oysters." There was some affectation of
roystering in all this; but it was a time of
social good-fellowship, and easy freedom of
manners in both sexes. At the dinners
there was much sentimental and bacchana-
lian singing; it was scarcely good manners
not to get a little tipsy; and to be laid
under the table by the compulsory bumper
was not to the discredit of a guest. Irving

used to like to repeat an anecdote of one of
his early friends, Henry Ogden, who had
been at one of these festive meetings. He
told Irving the next day that in going home
he had fallen through a grating which had
been carelessly left open, into a vault beneath. The solitude, he said, was rather
dismal at first, but several other of the
guests fell in, in the course of the evening,
and they had on the whole a pleasant night
of it.

These young gentlemen liked to be
thought " sad dogs." That they were less
abandoned than they pretended to be the
sequel of their lives shows: among Irving's
associates at this time who attained honorable consideration were John and Gouverneur
Kemble, Henry Brevoort, Henry Ogden,
James K. Paulding, and Peter Irving. The
saving influence for all of them was the refined households they frequented and the association of women who were high-spirited
without prudery, and who united purity
and simplicity with wit, vivacity, and charm
of manner. There is some pleasant correspondence between Irving and Miss Mary
Fairlie, a belle of the time, who married the

tragedian, Thomas A. Cooper; the "fascinating Fairlie," as Irving calls her, and the
Sophie Sparkle of the "Salmagundi." Irving's susceptibility to the charms and
graces of women — a susceptibility which
continued always fresh — was tempered and
ennobled by the most chivalrous admiration
for the sex as a whole.   He placed them on
an almost romantic pinnacle, and his actions
always conformed to his romantic ideal, although in his writings he sometimes adopts
the conventional satire which was more common fifty years ago than now.   In a letter
to Miss Fairlie, written from Richmond,
where he was attending the trial of Aaron
Burr, he expresses his exalted opinion of
the sex.   It was said in accounting for the
open sympathy of the ladies with the prisoner that Burr had always been a favorite
with them; "but I am not inclined," he
writes, "to account for it in so illiberal a
manner; it results from that merciful, that
heavenly disposition, implanted in the female bosom, which ever inclines in favor
of the accused and the unfortunate.   You
will smile at the high strain in which I
have indulged ; believe me, it is because I

feel it; and I love your sex ten times better than ever." [1]

Personally, Irving must have awakened a reciprocal admiration. A drawing by Vanderlyn, made in Paris in 1805, and a portrait by Jarvis in 1809, present him to us in the fresh bloom of manly beauty The face has an air of distinction and gen

[1] An amusing story in connection with this Richmond visit illustrates the romantic phase of Irving's character. Cooper, who was playing at the theatre, needed small-clothes for one of his parts; Irving lent him a pair, — knee-breeches being still worn, — and the actor carried them off to Baltimore. From that city he wrote that he had found in the pocket an emblem of love, a mysterious locket of hair in the shape of a heart. The history of it is curious: when Irving sojourned at Genoa he was much taken with the beauty of a young Italian lady, the wife of a Frenchman. He had never spoken with her, but one evening before his departure he picked up from the floor her handkerchief which she had dropped, and with more gallantry than honesty carried it off to Sicily. His pocket was picked of the precious relic while he was attending a religious function in Catania, and he wrote to his friend Storm, the consul at Genoa, deploring his loss. The consul communicated the sad misfortune to the lovely Bianca, for that was the lady's name, who thereupon sent him a lock of her hair, with the request that he would come to see her on his return. He never saw her again, but the lock of hair was inclosed in a locket and worn about his neck, in memory of a radiant vision that had crossed his path and vanished.

tle breeding; the refined lines, the poetic
chin, the sensitive mouth, the shapely nose,
the large dreamy eyes, the intellectual forehead, and the clustering brown locks are
our ideal of the author of the "Sketch-
Book" and the pilgrim in Spain. His biographer, Mr. Pierre M. Irving, has given
no description of his appearance; but a
relative, who saw much of our author in
his latter years, writes to me: "He had
dark gray eyes; a handsome straight nose,
which might perhaps be called large; a
broad, high, full forehead, and a small
mouth. I should call him of medium
height, about five feet eight and a half to
nine inches, and inclined to be a trifle stout.
There was no peculiarity about his voice;
but it was pleasant and had a good intona-
tion. His smile was exceedingly genial,
lighting up his whole face and rendering it
very attractive; while, if he were about to
say anything humorous, it would beam forth
from his eyes even before the words were
spoken. As a young man his face was exceedingly handsome, and his head was well
covered with dark hair; but from my earliest
recollection of him he wore neither whiskers

nor moustache, but a dark brown wig, which, although it made him look younger, concealed a beautifully shaped head." We can understand why he was a favorite in the society of Baltimore, Washington, Philadelphia, and Albany, as well as of New York, and why he liked to linger here and there, sipping the social sweets, like a man born to leisure and seemingly idle observation of life.

It was in the midst of these social successes, and just after his admission to the bar, that Irving gave the first decided evidence of the choice of a career. This was his association with his eldest brother, William, and Paulding in the production of " Salmagundi," a semi-monthly periodical, in small duodecimo sheets, which ran with tolerable regularity through twenty numbers, and stopped in full tide of success, with the whimsical indifference to the public which had characterized its every issue. Its declared purpose was " simply to instruct the young, reform the old, correct the town, and castigate the age." In manner and purpose it was an imitation of the " Spectator " and the " Citizen of the

World," and it must share the fate of all imitations; but its wit was not borrowed, and its humor was to some extent original; and so perfectly was it adapted to local conditions that it may be profitably read to-day as a not untrue reflection of the manners and spirit of the time and city. Its amusing audacity and complacent superiority, the mystery hanging about its writers, its affectation of indifference to praise or profit, its fearless criticism, lively wit, and irresponsible humor, piqued, puzzled, and delighted the town. From the first it was an immense success; it had a circulation in other cities, and many imitations of it sprung up. Notwithstanding many affectations and puerilities it is still readable to Americans. Of course, if it were offered now to the complex and sophisticated society of New York, it would fail to attract anything like the attention it received in the days of simplicity and literary dearth; but the same wit, insight, and literary art, informed with the modern spirit and turned upon the follies and "whim-whams" of the metropolis, would doubtless have a great measure of success. In Irving's contributions to it may be traced the germs of nearly everything that he did afterwards; in it he tried the various stops of his genius; he discovered his own power; his career was determined; thereafter it was only a question of energy or necessity.

In the summer of 1808 there were printed at Ballston-Spa— then the resort of fashion and the arena of flirtation — seven numbers of a duodecimo bagatelle in prose and verse, entitled " The Literary Picture Gallery and Admonitory Epistles to the Visitors of Ballston-Spa, by Simeon Senex, Esquire." This piece of summer nonsense is not referred to by any writer who has concerned himself about Irving's life, but there is reason to believe that he was a contributor to it if not the editor.[1]

In these yellow pages is a melancholy reflection of the gayety and gallantry of the Sans Souci hotel seventy years ago. In this " Picture Gallery," under the thin disguise of initials, are the portraits of well-known

[1] For these stray reminders of the old-time gayety of Ballston-Spa, I am indebted to J. Carson Brevoort, Esq., whose father was Irving's most intimate friend, and who told him that Irving had a hand in them.

belles of New York whose charms of person and graces of mind would make the present reader regret his tardy advent into this world, did not the "Admonitory Epistles," addressed to the same sex, remind him that the manners of seventy years ago left much to be desired. In respect of the habit of swearing, "Simeon" advises "Myra" that if ladies were to confine themselves to a single round oath, it would be quite sufficient; and he objects, when he is at the public table, to the conduct of his neighbor who carelessly took up "Simeon's" fork and used it as a tooth-pick. All this, no doubt, passed for wit in the beginning of the century. Punning, broad satire, exaggerated compliment, verse which has love for its theme and the "sweet bird of Venus" for its object, an affectation of gallantry and of *ennui*, with anecdotes of distinguished visitors, out of which the screaming fun has quite evaporated, make up the staple of these faded mementos of an ancient watering-place. Yet how much superior is our comedy of to-day? The beauty and the charms of the women of two generations ago exist only in tradition; perhaps we should give to the wit of that time equal admiration if none of it had been preserved.

Irving, notwithstanding the success of "Salmagundi," did not immediately devote himself to literature, nor seem to regard his achievements in it as anything more than aids to social distinction. He was then, as always, greatly influenced by his surroundings. These were unfavorable to literary pursuits. Politics was the attractive field for preferment and distinction; and it is more than probable that, even after the success of the Knickerbocker history, he would have drifted through life, half lawyer and half placeman, if the associations and stimulus of an old civilization, in his second European residence, had not fired his ambition. Like most young lawyers with little law and less clients, he began to dabble in local politics. The experiment was not much to his taste, and the association and work demanded, at that time, of a ward politician soon disgusted him. "We have toiled through the purgatory of an election," he writes to the fair Republican, Miss Fairlie, who rejoiced in the defeat he and the Federals had sustained : —

"What makes me the more outrageous is, that I got fairly drawn into the vortex, and before the third day was expired, I was as deep in mud and politics as ever a moderate gentleman would wish to be; and I drank beer with the multitude; and I talked hand-bill fashion with the demagogues; and I shook hands with the mob, whom my heart abhorreth. 'T is true, for the first two days I maintained my coolness and indifference. The first day I merely hunted for whim, character, and absurdity, according to my usual custom; the second day being rainy, I sat in the bar-room at the Seventh Ward, and read a volume of 'Galatea,' which I found on a shelf; but before I had got through a hundred pages, I had three or four good Feds sprawling round me on the floor, and another with his eyes half shut, leaning on my shoulder in the most affectionate manner, and spelling a page of the book as if it had been an electioneering hand-bill. But the third day — ah! then came the tug of war. My patriotism then blazed forth, and I determined to save my country! Oh, my friend, I have been in such holes and corners; such filthy nooks and filthy corners; sweep offices and oyster cellars! 'I have sworn brother to a leash of drawers, and can drink with any tinker in his own language during my life,' — faugh! I shall not be able to bear the smell of small beer and tobacco for a month to come. . . . Truly this saving one's country is a nauseous piece of business, and if patriotism is such a dirty virtue, — prythee, no more of it."

He unsuccessfully solicited some civil appointment at Albany, a very modest solicitation, which was never renewed, and which did not last long, for he was no sooner there than he was "disgusted by the servility and duplicity and rascality witnessed among the swarm of scrub politicians." There was a promising young artist at that time in Albany, and Irving wishes he were a man of wealth, to give him a helping hand; a few acts of munificence of this kind by rich nabobs, he breaks out, "would be more pleasing in the sight of Heaven, and more to the glory and advantage of their country, than building a dozen shingle church steeples, or buying a thousand venal votes at an election." This was in the "good old times!"

Although a Federalist, and, as he described himself, "an admirer of General Hamilton, and a partisan with him in politics," he accepted a retainer from Burr's friends in 1807, and attended his trial in Richmond, but more in the capacity of an

observer of the scene than a lawyer. He
did not share the prevalent opinion of Burr's
treason, and regarded him as a man so fallen
as to be shorn of the power to injure the
country, one for whom he could feel nothing
but compassion. That compassion, however,
he received only from the ladies of the city,
and the traits of female goodness manifested
then sunk deep into Irving's heart. Without pretending, he says, to decide on Burr's
innocence or guilt, "his situation is such as
should appeal eloquently to the feelings of
every generous bosom. Sorry am I to say
the reverse has been the fact: fallen, pro-
scribed, pre-judged, the cup of bitterness
has been administered to him with an un-
sparing hand. It has almost been considered
as culpable to evince toward him the least
sympathy or support; and many a hollow-
hearted caitiff have I seen, who basked in
the sunshine of his bounty while in power,
who now skulked from his side, and even
mingled among the most clamorous of his
enemies. . . . I bid him farewell with a
heavy heart, and he expressed with peculiar
warmth and feeling his sense of the interest
I had taken in his fate. I never felt in a

more melancholy mood than when I rode
from his solitary prison." This is a good
illustration of Irving's tender-heartedness;
but considering Burr's whole character, it
is altogether a womanish case of misplaced
sympathy with the cool slayer of Alexander
Hamilton.

CHAPTER V.

THE KNICKERBOCKER PERIOD.

NOT long after the discontinuance of "Salmagundi," Irving in connection with his brother Peter projected the work that was to make him famous. At first nothing more was intended than a satire upon the "Picture of New York," by Dr. Samuel Mitchell, just then published. It was begun as a mere burlesque upon pedantry and erudition, and was well advanced, when Peter was called by his business to Europe, and its completion was fortunately left to Washington. In his mind the idea expanded into a different conception. He condensed the mass of affected learning, which was their joint work, into five introductory chapters, — subsequently he said it would have been improved if it had been reduced to one, and it seems to me it would have been better if that one had been thrown away, — and finished "A History of New York," by Diedrich Knickerbocker, substantially as we now have it. This was in 1809, when Irving was twenty-six years old.

But before this humorous creation was completed, the author endured the terrible bereavement which was to color all his life. He had formed a deep and tender passion for Matilda Hoffman, the second daughter of Josiah Ogden Hoffman, in whose family he had long been on a footing of the most perfect intimacy, and his ardent love was fully reciprocated. He was restlessly casting about for some assured means of livelihood which would enable him to marry, and perhaps his distrust of a literary career was connected with this desire, when after a short illness Miss Hoffman died, in the eighteenth year of her age. Without being a dazzling beauty, she was lovely in person and mind, with most engaging manners, a refined sensibility, and a delicate and playful humor. The loss was a crushing blow to Irving, from the effects of which he never recovered, although time softened the bitterness of his grief into a tender and sacred memory. He could never bear to hear

her name spoken even by his most intimate friends, or any allusion to her. Thirty
years after her death, it happened one evening at the house of Mr. Hoffman, her father,
that a granddaughter was playing for Mr.
Irving, and in taking her music from the
drawer, a faded piece of embroidery was
brought forth. "Washington," said Mr.
Hoffman, picking it up, "this is a piece of
poor Matilda's workmanship." The effect
was electric. He had been talking in the
sprightliest mood before, but he sunk at
once into utter silence, and in a few mo-
ments got up and left the house.

After his death, in a private repository
of which he always kept the key, was found
a lovely miniature, a braid of fair hair, and
a slip of paper, on which was written in his
own hand, "Matilda Hoffman;" and with
these treasures were several pages of a
memorandum in ink long since faded. He
kept through life her Bible and Prayer
Book; they were placed nightly under his
pillow in the first days of anguish that followed her loss, and ever after they were the
inseparable companions of all his wanderings. In this memorandum — which was

written many years afterwards — we read the simple story of his love : —

" We saw each other every day, and I became excessively attached to her. Her shyness wore off by degrees. The more I saw of her the more I had reason to admire her. Her mind seemed to unfold leaf by leaf, and every time to discover new sweetness. Nobody knew her so well as I, for she was generally timid and silent; but I in a manner studied her excellence. Never did I meet with more intuitive rectitude of mind, more native delicacy, more exquisite propriety in word, thought, and action, than in this young creature. I am not exaggerating ; what I say was acknowledged by all who knew her. Her brilliant little sister used to say that people began by admiring her, but ended by loving Matilda. For my part, I idolized her. I felt at times rebuked by her superior delicacy and purity, and as if I was a coarse, unworthy being in comparison."

At this time Irving was much perplexed about his career. He had " a fatal propensity to belles-lettres ;" his repugnance to the law was such that his mind would not take hold of the study ; he anticipated nothing from legal pursuits or political employment; he was secretly writing the humorous history, but was altogether in a low-spirited and disheartened state. I quote again from the memorandum : —

" In the mean time I saw Matilda every day, and that helped to distract me. In the midst of this struggle and anxiety she was taken ill with a cold. Nothing was thought of it at first; but she grew rapidly worse, and fell into a consumption. I cannot tell you what I suffered. The ills that I have undergone in this life have been dealt out to me drop by drop, and I have tasted all their bitterness. I saw her fade rapidly away; beautiful, and more beautiful, and more angelical to the last. I was often by her bedside; and in her wandering state of mind she would talk to me with a sweet, natural, and affecting eloquence, that was overpowering. I saw more of the beauty of her mind in that delirious state than I had ever known before. Her malady was rapid in its career, and hurried her off in two months. Her dying struggles were painful and protracted. For three days and nights I did not leave the house, and scarcely slept. I was by her when she died; all the family were assembled round her, some praying, others weeping, for she was adored by them all. I was the last one she looked upon. I have told you as briefly as I could what, if I were to tell with all the incidents and feelings that accompanied it, would fill volumes. She was but about seventeen years old when she died.

"I cannot tell you what a horrid state of mind I was in for a long time. I seemed to care for nothing; the world was a blank to me. I abandoned all thoughts of the law. I went into the country, but could not bear solitude, yet could not endure society. There was a dismal horror continually in my mind, that made me fear to be alone. I had often to get up in the night, and seek the bedroom of my brother, as if the having a human being by me would relieve me from the frightful gloom of my own thoughts.

"Months elapsed before my mind would resume any tone; but the despondency I had suffered for a long time in the course of this attachment, and the anguish that attended its catastrophe, seemed to give a turn to my whole character, and throw some clouds into my disposition, which have ever since hung about it. When I became more calm and collected, I applied myself, by way of occupation, to the finishing of my work. I brought it to a close, as well as I could, and published it; but the time and circumstances in which it was produced rendered me always unable to look upon it with satisfaction. Still it took with the public, and gave me celebrity, as an original work was something remarkable and uncommon in America. I was noticed, caressed, and, for a time, elevated by the popularity I had gained. I found myself uncomfortable in my feelings in New York, and traveled about a little. Wherever I went I was overwhelmed with attentions; I was full of youth and animation, far different from the being I now am, and I was quite flushed with this early taste of public favor. Still, however, the career of gayety and notoriety soon palled on me. I seemed to drift about without aim or object, at the mercy of every breeze; my heart wanted anchorage. I was naturally susceptible, and tried to form other attachments, but my heart would not hold on; it would continually recur to what it had lost; and whenever there was a pause in the hurry of novelty and excitement, I would sink into dismal dejection. For years I could not talk on the subject of this hopeless regret; I could not even mention her name; but her image was continually before me, and I dreamt of her incessantly."

This memorandum, it subsequently appeared, was a letter, or a transcript of it, addressed to a married lady, Mrs. Foster, in which the story of his early love was related, in reply to her question why he had never married. It was in the year 1823,

the year after the publication of " Bracebridge Hall," while he sojourned in Dresden, that he became intimate with an English family residing there, named Foster,
and conceived for the daughter, Miss Emily
Foster, a warm friendship and perhaps a
deep attachment.   The letter itself, which
for the first time broke the guarded seclusion of Irving's heart, is evidence of the
tender confidence that existed between him
and this family.   That this intimacy would
have resulted in marriage, or an offer of
marriage, if the lady's affections had not
been preoccupied, the Fosters seem to have
believed.   In an unauthorized addition to
the " Life and Letters," inserted in the
English edition without the knowledge of
the American editor, with some such head-
ings as, " History of his First Love brought
to us, and returned," and " Irving's Second
Attachment," the Fosters tell the interesting story of Irving's life in Dresden, and
give many of his letters, and an account
of his intimacy with the family.   From this
account I quote : —

" Soon after this, Mr. Irving, who had again
for long felt ' the tenderest interest warm his
5

bosom, and finally enthrall his whole soul,' made one vigorous and valiant effort to free himself from a hopeless and consuming attachment. My mother counseled him, I believe, for the best, and he left Dresden on an expedition of several weeks into a country he had long wished to see, though, in the main, it disappointed him; and he started with young Colbourne (son of General Colbourne) as his companion. Some of his letters on this journey are before the public; and in the agitation and eagerness he there described, on receiving and opening letters from us, and the tenderness in his replies, — the longing to be once more in the little Pavilion, to which we had moved in the beginning of the summer, — the letters (though carefully guarded by the delicacy of her who intrusted them to the editor, and alone retained among many more calculated to lay bare his true feelings), even fragmentary as they are, point out the truth.

"Here is the key to the journey to Silesia, the return to Dresden, and, finally, to the journey from Dresden to Rotterdam in our company, first planned so as to part at Cassel, where Mr. Irving had intended to leave us and go down the Rhine, but subsequently could not find in his heart to part. Hence, after a night of pale and speechless melancholy, the gay, animated, happy countenance with which he sprang to our coach-

box to take his old seat on it, and accompany us
to Rotterdam. There even could he not part,
but joined us in the steamboat; and, after bearing us company as far as a boat could follow us,
at last tore himself away, to bury himself in
Paris, and try to work. . . .

"It was fortunate, perhaps, that this affection
was returned by the *warmest friendship* only,
since it was destined that the accomplishment
of his wishes was impossible, for many obstacles
which lay in his way; and it is with pleasure I
can truly say that in time he schooled himself to
view, also with friendship only, one who for
some time past has been the wife of another."

Upon the delicacy of this revelation the
biographer does not comment, but he says
that the idea that Irving thought of marriage at that time is utterly disproved by
the following passage from the very manuscript which he submitted to Mrs. Foster : —

"You wonder why I am not married. I have
shown you why I was not long since. When I
had sufficiently recovered from that loss, I became involved in ruin. It was not for a man
broken down in the world, to drag down any
woman to his paltry circumstances. I was too
proud to tolerate the idea of ever mending my

circumstances by matrimony. My time has now gone by; and I have growing claims upon my thoughts and upon my means, slender and precarious as they are. I feel as if I already had a family to think and provide for."

Upon the question of attachment and depression, Mr. Pierre Irving says : —

"While the editor does not question Mr. Irving's great enjoyment of his intercourse with the Fosters, or his deep regret at parting from them, he is too familiar with his occasional fits of depression to have drawn from their recurrence on his return to Paris any such inference as that to which the lady alludes. Indeed, his 'memorandum book' and letters show him to have had, at this time, sources of anxiety of quite a different nature. The allusion to his having 'to put once more to sea' evidently refers to his anxiety on returning to his literary pursuits, after a season of entire idleness."

It is not for us to question the judgment of the biographer, with his full knowledge of the circumstances and his long intimacy with his uncle; yet it is evident that Irving was seriously impressed at Dresden, and that he was very much unsettled until he drove away the impression by hard work with his pen ; and it would be nothing new in human nature and experience if he had for a time yielded to the attractions of loveliness and a most congenial companionship, and had returned again to an exclusive devotion to the image of the early loved and lost.

That Irving intended never to marry is an inference I cannot draw either from his fondness for the society of women, from his interest in the matrimonial projects of his friends and the gossip which has feminine attractions for its food, or from his letters to those who had his confidence. In a letter written from Birmingham, England, March 15, 1816, to his dear friend Henry Brevoort, who was permitted more than perhaps any other person to see his secret heart, he alludes, with gratification, to the report of the engagement of James Paulding, and then says : —

" It is what we must all come to at last. I see you are hankering after it, and I cónfess I have done so for a long time past. We are, however, past that period [Irving was thirty-two] when a man marries suddenly and inconsiderately. We may be longer making a choice, and consulting

the convenience and concurrence of easy circumstances, but we shall both come to it sooner or
later. I therefore recommend you to marry
without delay. You have sufficient means, connected with your knowledge and habits of business, to support a genteel establishment, and I
am certain that as soon as you are married you
will experience a change in your ideas. All
those vagabond, roving propensities will cease.
They are the offspring of idleness of mind and
a want of something to fix the feelings. You
are like a bark without an anchor, that drifts
about at the mercy of every vagrant breeze or
trifling eddy. Get a wife, and she 'll anchor you.
But don't marry a fool because she has a pretty
face, and don't seek after a great belle. Get
such a girl as Mary ——, or get her if you can;
though I am afraid she has still an unlucky kindness for poor ——, which will stand in the way
of her fortunes. I wish to God they were rich,
and married, and happy!"

The business reverses which befell the
Irving brothers, and which drove Washington to the toil of the pen, and cast upon him
heavy family responsibilities, defeated his
plans of domestic happiness in marriage.
It was in this same year, 1816, when the
fortunes of the firm were daily becoming

more dismal, that he wrote to Brevoort, upon the report that the latter was likely to remain a bachelor : " We are all selfish beings. Fortune by her tardy favors and capricious freaks seems to discourage all my matrimonial resolves, and if I am doomed to live an old bachelor, I am anxious to have good company. I cannot bear that all my old companions should launch away into the married state, and leave me alone to tread this desolate and sterile shore." And, in view of a possible life of scant fortune, he exclaims : " Thank Heaven, I was brought up in simple and inexpensive habits, and I have satisfied myself that, if need be, I can resume them without repining or inconvenience. Though I am willing, therefore, that Fortune should shower her blessings upon me, and think I can enjoy them as well as most men, yet I shall not make myself unhappy if she chooses to be scanty, and shall take the position allotted me with a cheerful and contented mind."

When Irving passed the winter of 1823 in the charming society of the Fosters at Dresden, the success of the " Sketch-Book " and " Bracebridge Hall " had given him as-

surance of his ability to live comfortably by
the use of his pen.

To resume. The preliminary announce-
ment of the History was a humorous and
skillful piece of advertising. Notices appeared in the newspapers of the disappear-
ance from his lodging of "a small, elderly
gentleman, dressed in an old black coat and
cocked hat, by the name of Knickerbocker."
Paragraphs from week to week, purporting
to be the result of inquiry, elicited the facts
that such an old gentleman had been seen
traveling north in the Albany stage; that
his name was Diedrich Knickerbocker; that
he went away owing his landlord; and that
he left behind a very curious kind of a written book, which would be sold to pay his bills
if he did not return. So skillfully was this
managed that one of the city officials was on
the point of offering a reward for the discovery of the missing Diedrich. This little man
in knee-breeches and cocked hat was the
germ of the whole "Knickerbocker legend,"
a fantastic creation, which in a manner took
the place of history, and stamped upon the
commercial metropolis of the New World
the indelible Knickerbocker name and char-

acter; and even now in the city it is an un-
defined patent of nobility to trace descent
from " an old Knickerbocker family."

The volume, which was first printed in
Philadelphia, was put forth as a grave history of the manners and government under
the Dutch rulers, and so far was the covert
humor carried that it was dedicated to the
New York Historical Society. Its success
was far beyond Irving's expectation. It
met with almost universal acclaim. It is
true that some of the old Dutch inhabitants
who sat down to its perusal, expecting to
read a veritable account of the exploits of
their ancestors, were puzzled by the indi-
rection of its commendation; and several
excellent old ladies of New York and Albany were in blazing indignation at the
ridicule put upon the old Dutch people,
and minded to ostracize the irreverent author from all social recognition. As late
as 1818, in an address before the Historical
Society, Mr. Gulian C. Verplanck, Irving's
friend, showed the deep irritation the book
had caused, by severe strictures on it as a
" coarse caricature." But the author's win-
ning ways soon dissipated the social cloud,

and even the Dutch critics were erelong
disarmed by the absence of all malice in the
gigantic humor of the composition. One
of the first foreigners to recognize the power
and humor of the book was Walter Scott.
"I have never," he wrote, "read anything
so closely resembling the style of Dean
Swift as the annals of Diedrich Knickerbocker. I have been employed these few
evenings in reading them aloud to Mrs. S.
and two ladies who are our guests, and our
sides have been absolutely sore with laughing. I think, too, there are passages which
indicate that the author possesses power of
a different kind, and has some touches which
remind me of Sterne."

The book is indeed an original creation,
and one of the few masterpieces of humor.
In spontaneity, freshness, breadth of conception, and joyous vigor, it belongs to the
spring-time of literature. It has entered
into the popular mind as no other American
book ever has, and it may be said to have
created a social realm which, with all its
whimsical conceit, has almost historical solidity. The Knickerbocker pantheon is almost as real as that of Olympus. The in-

troductory chapters are of that elephantine
facetiousness which pleased our great-grand-
fathers, but which is exceedingly tedious to
modern taste; and the humor of the book
occasionally has a breadth that is indelicate
to our apprehension, though it perhaps did
not shock our great-grandmothers. But,
notwithstanding these blemishes, I think
the work has more enduring qualities than
even the generation which it first delighted
gave it credit for. The world, however, it
must be owned, has scarcely yet the courage of its humor, and dullness still thinks
it necessary to apologize for anything amusing. There is little doubt that Irving himself supposed that his serious work was of
more consequence to the world.

It seems strange that after this success
Irving should have hesitated to adopt literature as his profession. But for two years,
and with leisure, he did nothing. He had
again some hope of political employment in
a small way; and at length he entered into
a mercantile partnership with his brothers,
which was to involve little work for him,
and a share of the profits that should assure
his support, and leave him free to follow

his fitful literary inclinations. Yet he seems
to have been mainly intent upon society and
the amusements of the passing hour, and,
without the spur of necessity to his literary
capacity, he yielded to the temptations of
indolence, and settled into the unpromising
position of a "man about town." Occasionally, the business of his firm and that of
other importing merchants being imperiled
by some threatened action of Congress, Irving was sent to Washington to look after
their interests. The leisurely progress he
always made to the capital through the
seductive society of Philadelphia and Baltimore did not promise much business dis-
patch. At the seat of government he was
certain to be involved in a whirl of gayety.
His letters from Washington are more occupied with the odd characters he met than
with the measures of legislation. These
visits greatly extended his acquaintance
with the leading men of the country; his
political leanings did not prevent an intimacy with the President's family, and Mrs.
Madison and he were sworn friends.

It was of the evening of his first arrival
in Washington that he writes: "I emerged

from dirt and darkness into the blazing splendor of Mrs. Madison's drawing-room. Here I was most graciously received; found a crowded collection of great and little men, of ugly old women and beautiful young ones, and in ten minutes was hand and glove with half the people in the assemblage. Mrs. Madison is a fine, portly, buxom dame, who has a smile and a pleasant word for everybody. Her sisters, Mrs. Cutts and Mrs. Washington, are like two merry wives of Windsor; but as to Jemmy Madison, — oh, poor Jemmy! — he is but a withered little apple-john."

Odd characters congregated then in Washington as now. One honest fellow, who, by faithful fagging at the heels of Congress, had obtained a profitable post under government, shook Irving heartily by the hand, and professed himself always happy to see anybody that came from New York; "somehow or another, it was *natteral* to him," being the place where he was *first* born. Another fellow-townsman was "endeavoring to obtain a deposit in the Mechanics' Bank, in case the United States Bank does not obtain a charter. He is as deep as usual; shakes his head and winks through his spectacles at everybody he meets. He swore to me the other day that he had not told anybody what his opinion was, — whether the bank ought to have a charter or not. Nobody in Washington knew what his opinion was — not one — nobody; he defied any one to say what it was — ' anybody — damn the one ! No, sir, nobody knows; ' and if he had added nobody cares, I believe honest —— would have been exactly in the right. Then there's his brother George : ' Damn that fellow, — knows eight or nine languages; yes, sir, nine languages, — Arabic, Spanish, Greek, Ital — And there's his wife, now, — she and Mrs. Madison are always together. Mrs. Madison has taken a great fancy to her little daughter. Only think, sir, that child is only six years old, and talks the Italian like a book, by —— ; little devil learnt it from an Italian servant, — damned clever fellow; lived with my brother George ten years. George says he would not part with him for all Tripoli,' " etc.

It was always difficult for Irving, in those days, to escape from the genial blandishments of Baltimore and Philadelphia. Writing to Brevoort from Philadelphia, March 16, 1811, he says: "The people of Baltimore are exceedingly social and hospitable to strangers, and I saw that if I once let myself get into the stream I should not be able to get out under a fortnight at least; so, being resolved to push home as expeditiously as was honorably possible, I resisted the world, the flesh, and the devil at Baltimore; and after three days' and nights' stout carousal, and a fourth's sickness, sorrow, and repentance, I hurried off from that sensual city."

Jarvis, the artist, was at that time the eccentric and elegant lion of society in Baltimore. "Jack Randolph" had recently sat to him for his portrait. "By the bye [the letter continues] that little 'hydra and chimera dire,' Jarvis, is in prodigious circulation at Baltimore. The gentlemen have all voted him a rare wag and most brilliant wit; and the ladies pronounce him one of the queerest, ugliest, most agreeable little creatures in the world. The consequence is there is not a ball, tea-party, concert, supper, or other private regale but that

Jarvis is the most conspicuous personage; and as to a dinner, they can no more do without him than they could without Friar John at the roystering revels of the renowned Pantagruel." Irving gives one of his *bon mots* which was industriously repeated at all the dinner tables, a profane sally, which seemed to tickle the Baltimoreans exceedingly. Being very much importuned to go to church, he resolutely refused, observing that it was the same thing whether he went or stayed at home. "If I don't go," said he, "the minister says I'll be d——d, and I'll be d——d if I do go."

This same letter contains a pretty picture, and the expression of Irving's habitual kindly regard for his fellow-men: —

"I was out visiting with Ann yesterday, and met that little assemblage of smiles and fascinations, Mary Jackson. She was bounding with youth, health, and innocence, and good humor. She had a pretty straw hat, tied under her chin with a pink ribbon, and looked like some little woodland nymph, just turned out by spring and fine weather. God bless her light heart, and grant it may never know care or sorrow! It's enough to cure spleen and melancholy only to look at her.

"Your familiar pictures of home made me extremely desirous again to be there. . . . I shall once more return to sober life, satisfied with having secured three months of sunshine in this valley of shadows and darkness. In this space of time I have seen considerable of the world, but I am sadly afraid I have not grown wiser thereby, inasmuch as it has generally been asserted by the sages of every age that wisdom consists in a knowledge of the wickedness of mankind, and the wiser a man grows the more discontented he becomes with those around him. Whereas, woe is me, I return in infinitely better humor with the world than I ever was before, and with a most melancholy good opinion and good will for the great mass of my fellow-creatures!"

Free intercourse with men of all parties, he thought, tends to divest a man's mind of party bigotry.

"One day [he writes] I am dining with a knot of honest, furious Federalists, who are damning all their opponents as a set of consummate scoundrels, panders of Bonaparte, etc. The next day I dine, perhaps, with some of the very men I have heard thus anathematized, and find them equally honest, warm, and indignant; and if I take their word for it, I had been dining the day

6

before with some of the greatest knaves in the
nation, men absolutely paid and suborned by the
British government."

His friends at this time attempted to get
him appointed secretary of legation to the
French mission, under Joel Barlow, then
minister, but he made no effort to secure
the place. Perhaps he was deterred by the
knowledge that the author of " The Colum-
biad " suspected him, though unjustly, of
some strictures on his great epic. He had
in mind a book of travel in his own country, in which he should sketch manners and
characters ; but nothing came of it. The
peril to trade involved in the War of 1812
gave him some forebodings, and aroused him
to exertion. He accepted the editorship of
a periodical called " Select Reviews," afterwards changed to the " Analectic Magazine," for which he wrote sketches, some of
which were afterwards put into the " Sketch-
Book," and several reviews and naval biographies. A brief biography of Thomas
Campbell was also written about this time,
as introductory to an edition of " Gertrude
of Wyoming." But the slight editorial care
required by the magazine was irksome to a

man who had an unconquerable repugnance
to all periodical labor.

In 1813 Francis Jeffrey made a visit to
the United States. Henry Brevoort, who
was then in London, wrote an anxious letter to Irving to impress him with the necessity of making much of Mr. Jeffrey. "It
is essential," he says, "that Jeffrey may
imbibe a just estimate of the United States
and its inhabitants; he goes out strongly
biased in our favor, and the influence of his
good opinion upon his return to this country will go far to efface the calumnies and
the absurdities that have been laid to our
charge by ignorant travelers. Persuade him
to visit Washington, and by all means to
see the Falls of Niagara." The impression
seems to have prevailed that if Englishmen
could be made to take a just view of the
Falls of Niagara the misunderstandings between the two countries would be reduced.
Peter Irving, who was then in Edinburgh,
was impressed with the brilliant talent of
the editor of the " Review," disguised as it
was by affectation, but he said he " would
not give the Minstrel for a wilderness of
Jeffreys."

The years from 1811 to 1815, when he went abroad for the second time, were passed by Irving in a sort of humble waiting on Providence. His letters to Brevoort during this period are full of the *ennui* of irresolute youth. He idled away weeks and months in indolent enjoyment in the country; he indulged his passion for the theatre when opportunity offered; and he began to be weary of a society which offered little stimulus to his mind. His was the temperament of the artist, and America at that time had little to evoke or to satisfy the artistic feeling. There were few pictures and no galleries; there was no music, except the amateur torture of strings which led the country dance, or the martial inflammation of fife and drum, or the sentimental dawdling here and there over the ancient harpsichord, with the songs of love, and the broad or pathetic staves and choruses of the convivial table; and there was no literary atmosphere.

After three months of indolent enjoyment in the winter and spring of 1811, Irving is complaining to Brevoort in June of the enervation of his social life: " I do want most deplorably to apply my mind to something that will arouse and animate it; for at present it is very indolent and relaxed, and I find it very difficult to shake off the lethargy that enthralls it. This makes me restless and dissatisfied with myself, and I am convinced I shall not feel comfortable and contented until my mind is fully employed. Pleasure is but a transient stimulus, and leaves the mind more enfeebled than before. Give me rugged toils, fierce disputation, wrangling controversy, harassing research,— give me anything that calls forth the energies of the mind; but for Heaven's sake shield me from those calms, those tranquil slumberings, those enervating triflings, those siren blandishments, that I have for some time indulged in, which lull the mind into complete inaction, which benumb its powers, and cost it such painful and humiliating struggles to regain its activity and independence !"

Irving at this time of life seemed always waiting by the pool for some angel to come and trouble the waters. To his correspondent, who was in the wilds of Michilimackinac, he continues to lament his morbid inability. The business in which his thriving brothers were engaged was the importation and sale of hardware and cutlery, and that spring his services were required at the " store." " By all the martyrs of Grub Street [he exclaims], I 'd sooner live in a garret, and starve into the bargain, than follow so sordid, dusty, and soul-killing a way of life, though certain it would make me as rich as old Crœsus, or John Jacob Astor himself ! " The sparkle of society was no more agreeable to him than the rattle of cutlery. " I have scarcely [he writes] seen anything of the ——s since your departure ; business and an amazing want of inclination have kept me from their threshold. Jim, that sly poacher, however, prowls about there, and vitrifies his heart by the furnace of their charms. I accompanied him there on Sunday evening last, and found the Lads and Miss Knox with them. S—— was in great spirits, and played the sparkler with such great success as to silence the whole of us excepting Jim, who was the *agreeable rattle* of the evening. God defend me from such vivacity as hers, in future, — such smart speeches without meaning, such bubble and squeak nonsense! I'd as lieve stand by a frying-pan for an hour and listen to the cooking of apple fritters. After two hours' dead silence and suffering on my part I made out to drag him off, and did not stop running until I was a mile from the house." Irving gives his correspondent graphic pictures of the social warfare in which he was engaged, the "host of rascally little tea-parties" in which he was entangled; and some of his portraits of the "divinities," the "blossoms," and the beauties of that day would make the subjects of them flutter with surprise in the church-yards where they lie. The writer was sated with the "tedious commonplace of fashionable society," and languishing to return to his books and his pen.

In March, 1812, in the shadow of the war and the depression of business, Irving was getting out a new edition of the "Knicker-bocker," which Inskeep was to publish, agreeing to pay $1,200 at six months for an edition of fifteen hundred. The modern publisher had not then arisen and acquired a proprietary right in the brains of the country, and the author made his bargains like an independent being who owned himself.

Irving's letters of this period are full of the gossip of the town and the matrimonial fate of his acquaintances. The fascinating Mary Fairlie is at length married to Cooper, the tragedian, with the opposition of her parents, after a dismal courtship and a cloudy prospect of happiness. "Goodhue is engaged to Miss Clarkson, the sister to the pretty one. The engagement suddenly took place as they walked from church on Christmas Day, and report says the action was shorter than any of our naval victories, for the lady struck on the first broadside." The war colored all social life and conversation. "This war [the letter is to Brevoort, who is in Europe] has completely changed the face of things here. You would scarcely recognize our old peaceful city. Nothing is talked of but armies, navies, battles, etc." The same phenomenon was witnessed then that was observed in the war for the Union: "Men who had loitered about, the hangers-on and encumbrances of society, have all at once risen to importance, and been the only useful men of the day."

The exploits of our young navy kept up the spirits of the country. There was great rejoicing when the captured frigate Macedonian was brought into New York, and was visited by the curious as she lay wind-bound above Hell Gate. "A superb dinner was given to the naval heroes, at which all the great eaters and drinkers of the city were present. It was the noblest entertainment of the kind I ever witnessed. On New Year's Eve a grand ball was likewise given, where there was a vast display of great and little people. The Livingstons were there in all their glory. Little Rule Britannia made a gallant appearance at the head of a train of beauties, among whom were the divine H——, who looked very inviting, and the little Taylor, who looked still more so. Britannia was gorgeously dressed in a queer kind of hat of stiff purple and silver stuff, that had marvelously the appearance of copper, and made us suppose that she had procured the real Mambrino helmet. Her dress was trimmed with what we simply mistook for scalps, and supposed it was in honor of the nation; but we blushed at our ignorance on discovering that it was a gorgeous trimming of marten tips. Would that some eminent furrier had been there to wonder and admire ! "

With a little business and a good deal of loitering, waiting upon the whim of his pen, Irving passed the weary months of the war. As late as August, 1814, he is still giving Brevoort, who has returned, and is at Rockaway Beach, the light gossip of the town. It was reported that Brevoort and Dennis had kept a journal of their foreign travel, "which is so exquisitely humorous that Mrs. Cooper, on only looking at the first word, fell into a fit of laughing that lasted half an hour." Irving is glad that he cannot find Brevoort's flute, which the latter requested should be sent to him : " I do not think it would be an innocent amusement for you, as no one has a right to entertain himself at the expense of others." In such dallying and badinage the months went on, affairs every day becoming more serious. Appended to a letter of September 9, 1814, is a list of twenty well-known mercantile houses that had failed within the preceding three weeks. Irving himself, shortly after this, enlisted in the war, and his letters thereafter breathe patriotic indignation at the insulting proposals of the British and their rumored attack on New York, and all his similes, even those having love for their subject, are martial and bellicose. Item: "The gallant Sam has fairly changed front, and, instead of laying siege to Douglas castle, has charged sword in hand, and carried little Cooper's entrenchments."

As a Federalist and an admirer of England, Irving had deplored the war, but his sympathies were not doubtful after it began, and the burning of the national Capitol by General Ross aroused him to an active participation in the struggle. He was descending the Hudson in a steamboat when the tidings first reached him. It was night, and the passengers had gone into the cabin, when a man came on board with the news, and in the darkness related the particulars: the burning of the President's house and government offices, and the destruction of the Capitol, with the library and public archives. In the momentary silence that followed, somebody raised his voice, and in a tone of complacent derision "wondered what *Jimmy* Madison would say now."

" Sir," cried Mr. Irving, in a burst of indignation that overcame his habitual shyness, " do you seize upon such a disaster only for a sneer? Let me tell you, sir, it is not now a question about *Jimmy* Madison or *Jimmy* Armstrong. The pride and honor of the nation are wounded; the country is insulted and disgraced by this barbarous success, and every loyal citizen would feel the ignominy and be earnest to avenge it." There was an outburst of applause, and the sneerer was silenced. " I could not see the fellow," said Mr. Irving, in relating the anecdote, " but I let fly at him in the dark."

The next day he offered his services to Governor Tompkins, and was made the governor's aid and military secretary, with the right to be addressed as Col. Washington Irving. He served only four months in this capacity, when Governor Tompkins was called to the session of the legislature at Albany. Irving intended to go to Washington and apply for a commission in the regular army, but he was detained at Philadelphia by the affairs of his magazine, until news came in February, 1815, of the close

of the war. In May of that year he embarked for England to visit his brother, intending only a short sojourn. He remained
abroad seventeen years.

CHAPTER VI.

LIFE IN EUROPE: LITERARY ACTIVITY.

WHEN Irving sailed from New York, it was with lively anticipations of witnessing the stirring events to follow the return of Bonaparte from Elba. When he reached Liverpool the curtain had fallen in Bonaparte's theatre. The first spectacle that met the traveler's eye was the mail coaches, darting through the streets, decked with laurel and bringing the news of Waterloo. As usual, Irving's sympathies were with the unfortunate. "I think," he says, writing of the exile of St. Helena, "the cabinet has acted with littleness toward him. In spite of all his misdeeds he is a noble fellow [*pace* Madame de Rémusat], and I am confident will eclipse, in the eyes of posterity, all the crowned wiseacres that have crushed him by their overwhelming confederacy. If anything could place the Prince Regent in a more ridiculous light, it is Bonaparte suing for his magnanimous protection. Every compliment paid to this bloated sensualist, this inflation of sack and sugar, turns to the keenest sarcasm."

After staying a week with his brother Peter, who was recovering from an indisposition, Irving went to Birmingham, the residence of his brother-in-law, Henry Van Wart, who had married his youngest sister, Sarah; and from thence to Sydenham, to visit Campbell. The poet was not at home. To Mrs. Campbell Irving expressed his regret that her husband did not attempt something on a grand scale.

"'It is unfortunate for Campbell,' said she, 'that he lives in the same age with Scott and Byron.' I asked why. 'Oh,' said she, 'they write so much and so rapidly. Mr. Campbell writes slowly, and it takes him some time to get under way; and just as he has fairly begun out comes one of their poems, that sets the world agog, and quite daunts him, so that he throws by his pen in despair.' I pointed out the essential difference in their kinds of poetry, and the qualities which insured perpetuity to that of her husband. 'You can't persuade Campbell of that,' said she. 'He is apt to undervalue his own

works, and to consider his own little lights put
out, whenever they come blazing out with their
great torches.'

"I repeated the conversation to Scott some time
afterward, and it drew forth a characteristic comment. 'Pooh!' said he, good humoredly; 'how
can Campbell mistake the matter so much? Poetry goes by quality, not by bulk. My poems are
mere cairngorms, wrought up, perhaps, with a cunning hand, and may pass well in the market as
long as cairngorms are the fashion; but they are
mere Scotch pebbles, after all. Now, Tom Campbell's are real diamonds, and diamonds of the
first water.'"

Returning to Birmingham, Irving made excursions to Kenilworth, Warwick, and Stratford-on-Avon, and a tour through Wales
with James Renwick, a young American of
great promise, who at the age of nineteen
had for a time filled the chair of natural
philosophy in Columbia College. He was
a son of Mrs. Jane Renwick, a charming
woman and a life-long friend of Irving, the
daughter of the Rev. Andrew Jeffrey, of
Lochmaben, Scotland, and famous in literature as "The Blue-Eyed Lassie" of Burns.
From another song, "When first I saw my

Jeanie's Face," which does not appear in the poet's collected works, the biographer quotes : —

> " But, sair, I doubt some happier swain
>   Has gained my Jeanie's favor ;
> If sae, may every bliss be hers,
>   Tho' I can never have her.

> " But gang she east, or gang she west,
>   'Twixt Nith and Tweed all over,
> While men have eyes, or ears, or taste,
>   She 'll always find a lover."

During Irving's protracted stay in England he did not by any means lose his interest in his beloved New York and the little society that was always dear to him. He relied upon his friend Brevoort to give him the news of the town, and in return he wrote long letters, — longer and more elaborate and formal than this generation has leisure to write or to read ; letters in which the writer laid himself out to be entertaining, and detailed his emotions and state of mind as faithfully as his travels and outward experiences.

No sooner was our war with England over than our navy began to make a reputation for itself in the Mediterranean. In his letter of August, 1815, Irving dwells with pride on Decatur's triumph over the Algerine pirates. He had just received a letter from that "worthy little tar, Jack Nicholson," dated on board the Flambeau, off Algiers. In it Nicholson says that " they fell in with and captured the admiral's ship, and *killed him*." Upon which Irving remarks : "As this is all that Jack's brevity will allow him to say on the subject, I should be at a loss to know whether they killed the admiral *before* or *after* his capture. The well-known humanity of our tars, however, induces me to the former conclusion." Nicholson, who has the honor of being alluded to in " The Croakers," was always a great favorite with Irving. His gallantry on shore was equal to his bravery at sea, but unfortunately his diffidence was greater than his gallantry; and while his susceptibility to female charms made him an easy and a frequent victim, he could never muster the courage to declare his passion. Upon one occasion, when he was desperately enamored of a lady whom he wished to marry, he got Irving to write for him a love-letter, containing an offer of his heart and hand. The enthralled but bashful sailor carried the letter in his pocket till it was worn out, without ever being able to summon pluck enough to deliver it.

While Irving was in Wales the Wiggins family and Madame Bonaparte passed through Birmingham, on their way to Cheltenham. Madame was still determined to assert her rights as a Bonaparte. Irving cannot help expressing sympathy for Wiggins: " The poor man has his hands full, with such a bevy of beautiful women under his charge, and all doubtless bent on pleasure and admiration." He hears, however, nothing further of her, except the newspapers mention her being at Cheltenham. " There are so many stars and comets thrown out of their orbits, and whirling about the world at present, that a little star like Madame Bonaparte attracts but slight attention, even though she draw after her so sparkling a tail as the Wiggins family." In another letter he exclaims: " The world is surely topsy-turvy, and its inhabitants shaken out of place: emperors and kings, statesmen and philosophers, Bonaparte, Alexander, Johnson, and the Wigginses, all strolling about the face of the earth."

The business of the Irving brothers soon absorbed all Washington's time and attention.   Peter was an invalid, and the whole weight of the perplexing affairs of the failing firm fell upon the one who detested business, and counted every hour lost that he gave to it.   His letters for two years are burdened with harassments in uncongenial details and unsuccessful struggles.   Liverpool, where he was compelled to pass most of his time, had few attractions for him, and his low spirits did not permit him to avail himself of such social advantages as were offered.   It seems that our enterprising countrymen flocked abroad, on the conclusion of peace.   "This place [writes Irving] swarms with Americans.   You never saw a more motley race of beings.   Some seem as if just from the woods, and yet stalk about the streets and public places with all the easy nonchalance that they would about their own villages.   Nothing can surpass the dauntless independence of all form, ceremony, fashion, or reputation of a downright, unsophisticated American.   Since the war, too, particularly, our lads seem to think they are ' the salt of the earth ' and the legitimate lords of creation. It would delight you to see some of them playing Indian when surrounded by the wonders and improvements of the Old World. It is impossible to match these fellows by anything this side the water. Let an Englishman talk of the battle of Waterloo, and they will immediately bring up New Orleans and Plattsburg. A thoroughbred, thoroughly appointed soldier is nothing to a Kentucky rifleman," etc., etc. In contrast to this sort of American was Charles King, who was then abroad : " Charles is exactly what an American should be abroad : frank, manly, and unaffected in his habits and manners, liberal and independent in his opinions, generous and unprejudiced in his sentiments towards other nations, but most loyally attached to his own." There was a provincial narrowness at that date and long after in America, which deprecated the open-minded patriotism of King and of Irving as it did the clear-sighted loyalty of Fenimore Cooper.

The most anxious time of Irving's life was the winter of 1815–16. The business worry increased. He was too jaded with the din of pounds, shillings, and pence to permit his pen to invent facts or to adorn realities. Nevertheless, he occasionally escapes from the tread-mill. In December he is in London, and entranced with the acting of Miss O'Neil. He thinks that Brevoort, if he saw her, would infallibly fall in love with this "divine perfection of a woman." He writes: "She is, to my eyes, the most soul-subduing actress I ever saw; I do not mean from her personal charms, which are great, but from the truth, force, and pathos of her acting. I have never been so completely melted, moved, and overcome at a theatre as by her performances. . . . Kean, the prodigy, is to me insufferable. He is vulgar, full of trick, and a complete mannerist. This is merely my opinion. He is cried up as a second Garrick, as a reformer of the stage, etc. It may be so. He may be right, and all the other actors wrong. This is certain: he is either very good or very bad. I think decidedly the latter; and I find no medium opinions concerning him. I am delighted with Young, who acts with great judgment, discrimination, and feeling. I think him much the best actor at present on the English stage. . . . In certain characters, such as may be classed with Macbeth, I do not think that Cooper has his equal in England. Young is the only actor I have seen who can compare with him." Later, Irving somewhat modified his opinion of Kean. He wrote to Brevoort: " Kean is a strange compound of merits and defects. His excellence consists in sudden and brilliant touches, in vivid exhibitions of passion and emotion. I do not think him a discriminating actor, or critical either at understanding or delineating character; but he produces effects which no other actor does."

In the summer of 1816, on his way from Liverpool to visit his sister's family at Birmingham, Irving tarried for a few days at a country place near Shrewsbury on the border of Wales, and while there encountered a character whose portrait is cleverly painted. It is interesting to compare this first sketch with the elaboration of it in the essay on The Angler in the " Sketch-Book."

" In one of our morning strolls [he writes, July 15th] along the banks of the Aleen, a beautiful little pastoral stream that rises among the Welsh mountains and throws itself into the Dee, we encountered a veteran angler of old Isaac Walton's school. He was an old Greenwich out-door pensioner, had lost one leg in the battle of Camperdown, had been in America in his youth, and indeed had been quite a rover, but for many years past had settled himself down in his native village, not far distant, where he lived very independently on his pension and some other small annual sums, amounting in all to about £40. His great hobby, and indeed the business of his life, was to angle. I found he had read Isaac Walton very attentively; he seemed to have imbibed all his simplicity of heart, contentment of mind, and fluency of tongue. We kept company with him almost the whole day, wandering along the beautiful banks of the river, admiring the ease and elegant dexterity with which the old fellow managed his angle, throwing the fly with unerring certainty at a great distance and among overhanging bushes, and waving it gracefully in the air, to keep it from entangling, as he stumped with his staff and wooden leg from one bend of the river to another. He kept up a continual flow of cheerful and entertaining talk, and what I particularly liked him for was, that though we tried every way to entrap him into some abuse of America and its inhabitants, there was no getting him to utter an ill-natured word concerning us. His whole conversation and deportment illustrated old Isaac's maxims as to the benign influence of angling over the human heart. . . . I ought to mention that he had two companions — one, a ragged, picturesque varlet, that had all the air of a veteran poacher, and I warrant would find any fish-pond in the neighborhood in the darkest night; the other was a disciple of the old philosopher, studying the art under him, and was son and heir apparent to the landlady of the village tavern."

A contrast to this pleasing picture is afforded by some character sketches at the little watering-place of Buxton, which our kindly observer visited the same year.

"At the hotel where we put up [he writes] we had a most singular and whimsical assemblage of beings. I don't know whether you were ever at an English watering-place, but if you have not been, you have missed the best opportunity of studying English oddities, both moral and physical. I no longer wonder at the English being such excellent caricaturists, they have such an inexhaustible number and variety of subjects to study from. The only care should be not to follow fact too closely, for I 'll swear I have met

with characters and figures that would be con-
demned as extravagant, if faithfully delineated
by pen or pencil. At a watering-place like Buxton, where people really resort for health, you see
the great tendency of the English to run into
excrescences and bloat out into grotesque de-
formities. As to noses, I say nothing of them,
though we had every variety: some snubbed and
turned up, with distended nostrils, like a dormer
window on the roof of a house; others convex
and twisted like a buck-handled knife; and others
magnificently efflorescent, like a full-blown cauli-
flower. But as to the persons that were attached
to these noses, fancy any distortion, protuber-
ance, and fungous embellishment that can be produced in the human form by high and gross feeding, by the bloating operations of malt liquors,
and by the rheumy influence of a damp, foggy,
vaporous climate. One old fellow was an exception to this, for instead of acquiring that expansion and sponginess to which old people are prone
in this country, from the long course of internal
and external soakage they experience, he had
grown dry and stiff in the process of years. The
skin of his face had so shrunk away that he could
not close eyes or mouth — the latter, therefore,
stood on a perpetual ghastly grin, and the former
on an incessant stare. He had but one service-
able joint in his body, which was at the bottom

of the backbone, and that creaked and grated whenever he bent. He could not raise his feet from the ground, but skated along the drawing-room carpet whenever he wished to ring the bell. The only sign of moisture in his whole body was a pellucid drop that I occasionally noticed on the end of a long, dry nose. He used generally to shuffle about in company with a little fellow that was fat on one side and lean on the other. That is to say, he was warped on one side as if he had been scorched before the fire; he had a wry neck, which made his head lean on one shoulder; his hair was smugly powdered, and he had a round, smirking, smiling, apple face, with a bloom on it like that of a frost-bitten leaf in autumn. We had an old, fat general by the name of Trotter, who had, I suspect, been promoted to his high rank to get him out of the way of more able and active officers, being an instance that a man may occasionally rise in the world through absolute lack of merit. I could not help watching the movements of this redoubtable old Hero, who, I'll warrant, has been the champion and safeguard of half the garrison towns in England, and fancying to myself how Bonaparte would have delighted in having such toast-and-butter generals to deal with. This old cad is doubtless a sample of those generals that flourished in the old military school, when armies would manœuvre and watch each other for months; now and then have a desperate skirmish, and, after marching and countermarching about the 'Low Countries' through a glorious campaign, retire on the first pinch of cold weather into snug winter quarters in some fat Flemish town, and eat and drink and fiddle through the winter. Boney must have sadly disconcerted the comfortable system of these old warriors by the harrowing, restless, cut-and-slash mode of warfare that he introduced. He has put an end to all the old *carte and tierce* system in which the cavaliers of the old school fought so decorously, as it were with a small sword in one hand and a chapeau bras in the other. During his career there has been a sad laying on the shelf of old generals who could not keep up with the hurry, the fierceness and dashing of the new system; and among the number I presume has been my worthy house-mate, old Trotter. The old gentleman, in spite of his warlike title, had a most pacific appearance. He was large and fat, with a broad, hazy, muffin face, a sleepy eye, and a full double chin. He had a deep ravine from each corner of his mouth, not occasioned by any irascible contraction of the muscles, but apparently the deep-worn channels of two rivulets of gravy that oozed out from the huge mouthfuls that he masticated. But I forbear to dwell on the odd beings that were congregated together in one hotel. I have been thus prolix about the old general because you desired me in one of your letters to give you ample details whenever I happened to be in company with the 'great and glorious,' and old Trotter is more deserving of the epithet than any of the personages I have lately encountered."

It was at the same resort of fashion and disease that Irving observed a phenomenon upon which Brevoort had commented as beginning to be noticeable in America.

" Your account [he writes] of the brevity of the old lady's nether garments distresses me. . . . I cannot help observing that this fashion of short skirts must have been invented by the French ladies as a complete trick upon John Bull's 'woman-folk.' It was introduced just at the time the English flocked in such crowds to Paris. The French women, you know, are remarkable for pretty feet and ankles, and can display them in perfect security. The English are remarkable for the contrary. Seeing the proneness of the English women to follow French fashions, they therefore led them into this disastrous one, and sent them home with their petticoats up to their knees, exhibiting such a variety of sturdy little legs as would have afforded Hogarth an ample choice to match one of his assemblages of queer

heads. It is really a great source of curiosity
and amusement on the promenade of a watering-
place to observe the little sturdy English women,
trudging about in their stout leather shoes, and
to study the various ' understandings' betrayed
to view by this mischievous fashion."

The years passed rather wearily in England. Peter continued to be an invalid,
and Washington himself, never robust, felt
the pressure more and more of the irksome
and unprosperous business affairs. Of his
own want of health, however, he never com-
plains; he maintains a patient spirit in the
ill turns of fortune, and his impatience in
the business complications is that of a man
hindered from his proper career. The
times were depressing.

" In America [he writes to Brevoort] you
have financial difficulties, the embarrassments of
trade, the distress of merchants, but here you
have what is far worse, the distress of the poor
— not merely mental sufferings, but the absolute miseries of nature : hunger, nakedness,
wretchedness of all kinds that the laboring people in this country are liable to. In the best of
times they do but subsist, but in adverse times
they starve. How the country is to extricate it-

self from its present embarrassment, how it is to escape from the poverty that seems to be overwhelming it, and how the government is to quiet the multitudes that are already turbulent and clamorous, and are yet but in the beginning of their real miseries, I cannot conceive."

The embarrassments of the agricultural and laboring classes and of the government were as serious in 1816 as they have again become in 1881.

During 1817 Irving was mostly in the depths of gloom, a prey to the monotony of life and torpidity of intellect. Rays of sunlight pierce the clouds occasionally. The Van Wart household at Birmingham was a frequent refuge for him, and we have pretty pictures of the domestic life there; glimpses of Old Parr, whose reputation as a gourmand was only second to his fame as a Grecian, and of that delightful genius, the Rev. Rann Kennedy, who might have been famous if he had ever committed to paper the long poems that he carried about in his head, and the engaging sight of Irving playing the flute for the little Van Warts to dance. During the holidays Irving paid another visit to the haunts of Isaac Walton, and his

description of the adventures and mishaps
of a pleasure party on the banks of the
Dove suggest that the incorrigible bachelor
was still sensitive to the allurements of life,
and liable to wander over the " dead-line "
of matrimonial danger.   He confesses that
he was all day in Elysium.   " When we
had descended from the last precipice," he
says, "and come to where the Dove flowed
musically through a verdant meadow — then
— fancy me, oh, thou ' sweetest of poets,'
wandering by the course of this romantic
stream — a lovely girl hanging on my arm,
pointing out the beauties of the surrounding scenery, and repeating in the most dul-
cet voice tracts of heaven-born poetry.   If
a strawberry smothered in cream has any
consciousness of its delicious situation, it
must feel as I felt at that moment."   Indeed, the letters of this doleful year are
enlivened by so many references to the
graces and attractions of lovely women, seen
and remembered, that insensibility cannot
be attributed to the author of the " Sketch-
Book."

The death of Irving's mother in the
spring of 1817 determined him to remain

another year abroad. Business did not improve. His brother-in-law Van Wart called a meeting of his creditors, the Irving brothers floundered on into greater depths of embarrassment, and Washington, who could not think of returning home to face poverty in New York, began to revolve a plan that would give him a scanty but sufficient support. The idea of the "Sketch-Book" was in his mind. He had as yet made few literary acquaintances in England. It is an illustration of the warping effect of friendship upon the critical faculty that his opinion of Moore at this time was totally changed by subsequent intimacy. At a later date the two authors became warm friends and mutual admirers of each other's productions. In June, 1817, "Lalla Rookh" was just from the press, and Irving writes to Brevoort: "Moore's new poem is just out. I have not sent it to you, for it is dear and worthless. It is written in the most effeminate taste, and fit only to delight boarding-school girls and lads of nineteen just in their first loves. Moore should have kept to songs and epigrammatic conceits. His stream of intellect is too small to bear expansion — it spreads

8

into mere surface." Too much cream for the strawberry!

Notwithstanding business harassments in the summer and fall of 1817 he found time for some wandering about the island; he was occasionally in London, dining at Murray's, where he made the acquaintance of the elder D'Israeli and other men of letters (one of his notes of a dinner at Murray's is this: "Lord Byron told Murray that he was much happier after breaking with Lady Byron — he hated this still, quiet life"); he was publishing a new edition of the "Knickerbocker," illustrated by Leslie and Allston; and we find him at home in the friendly and brilliant society of Edinburgh; both the magazine publishers, Constable and Blackwood, were very civil to him, and Mr. Jeffrey (Mrs. Renwick was his sister) was very attentive; and he passed some days with Walter Scott, whose home life he so agreeably describes in his sketch of "Abbotsford." He looked back longingly to the happy hours there (he writes to his brother): "Scott reading, occasionally, from 'Prince Arthur'; telling border stories or characteristic anecdotes; Sophy Scott

singing with charming *naïveté* a little border song; the rest of the family disposed in
listening groups, while greyhounds, span-
iels, and cats bask in unbounded indulgence
before the fire. Everything about Scott is
perfect character and picture."

In the beginning of 1818 the business affairs of the brothers became so irretrievably
involved that Peter and Washington went
through the humiliating experience of taking the bankrupt act. Washington's connection with the concern was little more
than nominal, and he felt small anxiety for
himself, and was eager to escape from an
occupation which had taken all the elasticity out of his mind. But on account of his
brothers, in this dismal wreck of a family
connection, his soul was steeped in bitterness. Pending the proceedings of the com-
missioners, he shut himself up day and night
to the study of German, and while waiting
for the examination used to walk up and
down the room, conning over the German
verbs.

In August he went up to London and
cast himself irrevocably upon the fortune of
his pen. He had accumulated some mate

rials, and upon these he set to work. Efforts were made at home to procure for him the position of Secretary of Legation in London, which drew from him the remark, when they came to his knowledge, that he did not like to have his name hackneyed about among the office-seekers in Washington. Subsequently his brother William wrote him that Commodore Decatur was keeping open for him the office of Chief Clerk in the Navy Department. To the mortification and chagrin of his brothers, Washington declined the position. He was resolved to enter upon no duties that would interfere with his literary pursuits.

This resolution, which exhibited a modest confidence in his own powers, and the energy with which he threw himself into his career, showed the fibre of the man. Suddenly, by the reverse of fortune, he who had been regarded as merely the ornamental genius of the family became its stay and support. If he had accepted the aid of his brothers, during the experimental period of his life, in the loving spirit of confidence in which it was given, he was not less ready to reverse the relations when the time came;

the delicacy with which his assistance was
rendered, the scrupulous care taken to con-
vey the feeling that his brothers were doing
him a continued favor in sharing his good
fortune, and their own unjealous acceptance
of what they would as freely have given if
circumstances had been different, form one
of the pleasantest instances of brotherly
concord and self-abnegation. I know nothing more admirable than the life-long relations of this talented and sincere family.

Before the "Sketch-Book" was launched,
and while Irving was casting about for the
means of livelihood, Walter Scott urged
him to take the editorship of an Anti-Ja-
cobin periodical in Edinburgh. This he declined because he had no taste for politics,
and because he was averse to stated, routine literary work. Subsequently Mr. Murray offered him a salary of a thousand
guineas to edit a periodical to be published
by himself. This was declined, as also was
another offer to contribute to the "London
Quarterly" with the liberal pay of one hundred guineas an article. For the "Quarterly" he would not write, because, he says,
"it has always been so hostile to my coun-

try, I cannot draw a pen in its service."
This is worthy of note in view of a charge
made afterwards, when he was attacked
for his English sympathies, that he was a
frequent contributor to this anti-American
review. His sole contributions to it were
a gratuitous review of the book of an American author, and an explanatory article,
written at the desire of his publisher, on
the "Conquest of Granada." It is not necessary to dwell upon the small scandal about
Irving's un-American feeling. If there was
ever a man who loved his country and was
proud of it; whose broad, deep, and strong
patriotism did not need the saliency of ignorant partisanship, it was Washington Irving. He was like his namesake an American, and with the same pure loyalty and
unpartisan candor.

The first number of the "Sketch-Book"
was published in America in May, 1819.
Irving was then thirty-six years old. The
series was not completed till September,
1820. The first installment was carried
mainly by two papers, "The Wife" and
"Rip Van Winkle:" the one full of tender
pathos that touched all hearts, because it

was recognized as a genuine expression of
the author's nature; and the other a happy
effort of imaginative humor, — one of those
strokes of genius that recreate the world
and clothe it with the unfading hues of romance ; the theme was an old-world echo,
transformed by genius into a primal story
that will endure as long as the Hudson flows
through its mountains to the sea. A great
artist can paint a great picture on a small
canvas.

The " Sketch-Book " created a sensation
in America, and the echo of it was not long
in reaching England. The general chorus
of approval and the rapid sale surprised Irving, and sent his spirits up, but success
had the effect on him that it always has on
a fine nature. He writes to Leslie : " Now
you suppose I am all on the alert, and full
of spirit and excitement. No such thing. I
am just as good for nothing as ever I was ;
and, indeed, have been flurried and put out
of my way by these puffings. I feel something as I suppose you did when your picture met with success, — anxious to do something better, and at a loss what to do."

It was with much misgiving that Irving

made this venture. "I feel great diffidence," he writes Brevoort, March 3, 1819, "about this reappearance in literature. I am conscious of my imperfections, and my mind has been for a long time past so pressed upon and agitated by various cares and anxieties, that I fear it has lost much of its cheerfulness and some of its activity. I have attempted no lofty theme, nor sought to look wise and learned, which appears to be very much the fashion among our American writers at present. I have preferred addressing myself to the feelings and fancy of the reader more than to his judgment. My writings may appear, therefore, light and trifling in our country of philosophers and politicians. But if they possess merit in the class of literature to which they belong, it is all to which I aspire in the work. I seek only to blow a flute accompaniment in the national concert, and leave others to play the fiddle and French-horn." This diffidence was not assumed. All through his career, a breath of criticism ever so slight acted temporarily like a hoar-frost upon his productive power. He always saw reasons to take sides with his critic. Speak-

ing of "vanity" in a letter of March, 1820,
when Scott and Lockhart and all the Reviews were in a full chorus of acclaim, he
says : " I wish I did possess more of it, but
it seems my curse at present to have anything but confidence in myself or pleasure
in anything I have written."

In a similar strain he had written, in
September, 1819, on the news of the cor-
dial reception of the "Sketch-Book" in
America : —

"The manner in which the work has been received, and the eulogiums that have been passed
upon it in the American papers and periodical
works, have completely overwhelmed me. They
go far, *far* beyond my most sanguine expectations, and indeed are expressed with such peculiar warmth and kindness as to affect me in the
tenderest manner. The receipt of your letter,
and the reading of some of the criticisms this
morning, have rendered me nervous for the whole
day. I feel almost appalled by such success, and
fearful that it cannot be real, or that it is not
fully merited, or that I shall not act up to the
expectations that may be formed. We are whim-
sically constituted beings. I had got out of conceit of all that I had written, and considered it
very questionable stuff; and now that it is so ex-

travagantly bepraised, I begin to feel afraid that
I shall not do as well again.   However, we shall
see as we get on.   As yet I am extremely irregular and precarious in my fits of composition.   The
least thing puts me out of the vein, and even
applause flurries me and prevents my writing,
though of course it will ultimately be a stimulus. . . .

" I have been somewhat touched by the manner in which my writings have been noticed in
the ' Evening Post.'   I had considered Coleman
as cherishing an ill-will toward me, and, to tell
the truth, have not always been the most courteous in my opinions concerning him.   It is a painful thing either to dislike others or to fancy they
dislike us, and I have felt both pleasure and self-
reproach at finding myself so mistaken with respect to Mr. Coleman.   I like to out with a
good feeling as soon as it rises, and so I have
dropt Coleman a line on the subject.

" I hope you will not attribute all this sensibility to the kind reception I have met to an
author's vanity.   I am sure it proceeds from
very different sources.   Vanity could not bring
the tears into my eyes as they have been brought
by the kindness of my countrymen.   I have felt
cast down, blighted, and broken-spirited, and
these sudden rays of sunshine agitate me more
than they revive me.   I hope — I hope I may

yet do something more worthy of the appreciation lavished on me."

Irving had not contemplated publishing in England, but the papers began to be reprinted, and he was obliged to protect himself. He offered the sketches to Murray, the princely publisher, who afterwards dealt so liberally with him, but the venture was declined in a civil note, written in that charming phraseology with which authors are familiar, but which they would in vain seek to imitate. Irving afterwards greatly prized this letter. He undertook the risks of the publication himself, and the book sold well, although " written by an author the public knew nothing of, and published by a bookseller who was going to ruin." In a few months Murray, who was thereafter proud to be Irving's publisher, undertook the publication of the two volumes of the "Sketch-Book," and also of the " Knickerbocker " history, which Mr. Lockhart had just been warmly praising in " Blackwood's." Indeed, he bought the copyright of the "Sketch-Book" for two hundred pounds. The time for the publisher's complaisance had arrived sooner even than Scott

predicted in one of his kindly letters to Irving, " when

> ' Your name is up and may go
> From Toledo to Madrid.' "

Irving passed five years in England.
Once recognized by the literary world,
whatever was best in the society of letters
and of fashion was open to him. He was
a welcome guest in the best London houses,
where he met the foremost literary personages of the time, and established most
cordial relations with many of them; not to
speak of statesmen, soldiers, and men and
women of fashion, there were the elder D'Israeli, Southey, Campbell, Hallam, Gifford,
Milman, Foscolo, Rogers, Scott, and Belzoni fresh from his Egyptian explorations.
In Irving's letters this old society passes
in review: Murray's drawing-rooms; the
amusing blue-stocking coteries of fashion of
which Lady Caroline Lamb was a pro-
moter; the Countess of Besborough's, at
whose house The Duke could be seen; the
Wimbledon country seat of Lord and Lady
Spence; Belzoni, a giant of six feet five,
the centre of a group of eager auditors of
the Egyptian marvels; Hallam, affable and

unpretending, and a copious talker ; Gifford,
a small, shriveled, deformed man of sixty,
with something of a humped back, eyes
that diverge, and a large mouth, reclining on
a sofa, propped up by cushions, with none of
the petulance that you would expect from
his Review, but a mild, simple, unassum-
ing man, — he it is who prunes the contributions and takes the sting out of them
(one would like to have seen them before
the sting was taken out) ; and Scott, the
right honest-hearted, entering into the passing scene with the hearty enjoyment of a
child, to whom literature seems a sport
rather than a labor or ambition, an author
void of all the petulance, egotism, and peculiarities of the craft. We have Moore's
authority for saying that the literary dinner
described in the " The Tales of a Traveller,"
whimsical as it seems and pervaded by the
conventional notion of the relations of publishers and authors, had a personal foundation. Irving's satire of both has always
the old-time Grub Street flavor, or at least
the reminiscent tone, which is, by the way,
quite characteristic of nearly everything that
he wrote about England. He was always

a little in the past tense. Buckthorne's advice to his friend is, never to be eloquent to an author except in praise of his own works, or, what is nearly as acceptable, in disparagement of the work of his contemporaries. "If ever he speaks favorably of the productions of a particular friend, dissent boldly from him; pronounce his friend to be a blockhead; never fear his being vexed. Much as people speak of the irritability of authors, I never found one to take offense at such contradictions. No, no, sir, authors are particularly candid in admitting the faults of their friends." At the dinner Buckthorne explains the geographical boundaries in the land of literature: you may judge tolerably well of an author's popularity by the wine his bookseller gives him. "An author crosses the port line about the third edition, and gets into claret; and when he has reached the sixth or seventh, he may revel in champagne and burgundy." The two ends of the table were occupied by the two partners, one of whom laughed at the clever things said by the poet, while the other maintained his sedateness and kept on carving. "His gravity was explained to us by my friend Buckthorne. He informed me that the concerns of the house were admirably distributed among the partners. Thus, for instance, said he, the grave gentleman is the carving partner, who attends to the joints; and the other is the laughing partner, who attends to the jokes." If any of the jokes from the lower end of the table reached the upper end, they seldom produced much effect. "Even the laughing partner did not think it necessary to honor them with a smile; which my neighbor Buckthorne accounted for by informing me that there was a certain degree of popularity to be obtained before a bookseller could afford to laugh at an author's jokes."

In August, 1820, we find Irving in Paris, where his reputation secured him a hearty welcome: he was often at the Cannings' and at Lord Holland's; Talma, then the king of the stage, became his friend, and there he made the acquaintance of Thomas Moore, which ripened into a familiar and lasting friendship. The two men were drawn to each other; Irving greatly admired the "noble-hearted, manly, spirited little fellow, with a mind as generous as his fancy is brilliant." Talma was playing Hamlet to overflowing houses, which hung on his actions with breathless attention, or broke into ungovernable applause; ladies were carried fainting from the boxes. The actor is described as short in stature, rather inclined to fat, with a large face and a thick neck; his eyes are bluish, and have a peculiar cast in them at times. He said to Irving that he thought the French character much changed — graver; the day of the classic drama, mere declamation and fine language, had gone by; the Revolution had taught them to demand real life, incident, passion, character. Irving's life in Paris was gay enough, and seriously interfered with his literary projects. He had the fortunes of his brother Peter on his mind also, and invested his earnings, then and for some years after, in enterprises for his benefit that ended in disappointment.

The " Sketch-Book " was making a great fame for him in England. Jeffrey, in the " Edinburgh Review," paid it a most flattering tribute, and even the savage " Quarterly " praised it. A rumor attributed it to Scott, who was always masquerading; at least, it was said, he might have revised it, and should have the credit of its exquisite style. This led to a sprightly correspondence between Lady Littleton, the daughter of Earl Spencer, one of the most accomplished and lovely women of England, and Benjamin Rush, Minister to the Court of St. James, in the course of which Mr. Rush suggested the propriety of giving out under his official seal that Irving was the author of " Waverley." " Geoffrey Crayon is the most fashionable fellow of the day," wrote the painter Leslie. Lord Byron, in a letter to Murray, underscored his admiration of the author, and subsequently said to an American : " His Crayon,— I know it by heart ; at least, there is not a passage that I cannot refer to immediately." And afterwards he wrote to Moore, " His writings are my delight." There seemed to be, as some one wrote, "a kind of conspiracy to hoist him over the heads of his contemporaries." Perhaps the most satisfactory evidence of his popularity was his publisher's enthusiasm. The publisher is an infallible contemporary barometer.

9

It is worthy of note that an American should have captivated public attention at the moment when Scott and Byron were the idols of the English-reading world.

In the following year Irving was again in England, visiting his sister in Birmingham, and tasting moderately the delights of London. He was, indeed, something of an invalid. An eruptive malady,— the revenge of nature, perhaps, for defeat in her earlier attack on his lungs,— appearing in his ankles, incapacitated him for walking, tormented him at intervals, so that literary composition was impossible, sent him on pilgrimages to curative springs, and on journeys undertaken for distraction and amusement, in which all work except that of seeing and absorbing material had to be postponed. He was subject to this recurring invalidism all his life, and we must regard a good part of the work he did as a pure triumph of determination over physical discouragement. This year the fruits of his interrupted labor appeared in " Bracebridge Hall," a volume that was well received, but did not add much to his reputation, though it contained " Dolph Heyliger," one of his

most characteristic Dutch stories, and the
" Stout Gentleman," one of his daintiest
and most artistic bits of restrained humor.[1]

Irving sought relief from his malady by
an extended tour in Germany. He sojourned some time in Dresden, whither his
reputation had preceded him, and where he
was cordially and familiarly received, not
only by the foreign residents, but at the
prim and antiquated little court of King
Frederick Augustus and Queen Amalia. Of
Irving at this time Mrs. Emily Fuller (*née*
Foster), whose relations with him have been
referred to, wrote in 1860 : —

" He was thoroughly a gentleman, not merely
in external manners and look, but to the inner-
most fibres and core of his heart : sweet-tem-
pered, gentle, fastidious, sensitive, and gifted with
the warmest affections; the most delightful and

---

[1] I was once [says his biographer] reading aloud in his
presence a very flattering review of his works, which had
been sent him by the critic in 1848, and smiled as I came
to this sentence : " His most comical pieces have always
a serious end in view." " You laugh," said he, with that
air of whimsical significance so natural to him, " but it
is true. I have kept that to myself hitherto, but that
man has found me out. He has detected the moral of
the *Stout Gentleman.*"

invariably interesting companion; gay and full of humor, even in spite of occasional fits of melancholy, which he was, however, seldom subject to when with those he liked; a gift of conversation that flowed like a full river in sunshine,—bright, easy, and abundant."

Those were pleasant days at Dresden, filled up with the society of bright and warm-hearted people, varied by royal boar hunts, stiff ceremonies at the little court, tableaux, and private theatricals, yet tinged with a certain melancholy, partly constitutional, that appears in most of his letters. His mind was too unsettled for much composition. He had little self-confidence, and was easily put out by a breath of adverse criticism. At intervals he would come to the Fosters to read a manuscript of his own.

"On these occasions strict orders were given that no visitor should be admitted till the last word had been read, and the whole praised or criticised, as the case may be. Of criticism, however, we were very spare, as a slight word would put him out of conceit of a whole work. One of the best things he has published was thrown aside, unfinished, for years, because the friend to whom he read it, happening, unfortunately, not to be well, and sleepy, did not seem to take the interest in it he expected. Too easily discouraged, it was not till the latter part of his career that he ever appreciated himself as an author. One condemning whisper sounded louder in his ear than the plaudits of thousands."

This from Miss Emily Foster, who elsewhere notes his kindliness in observing life : —

" Some persons, in looking upon life, view it as they would view a picture, with a stern and criticising eye. He also looks upon life as a picture, but to catch its beauties, its lights, — not its defects and shadows. On the former he loves to dwell. He has a wonderful knack at shutting his eyes to the sinister side of anything. Never beat a more kindly heart than his ; alive to the sorrows, but not to the faults, of his friends, but doubly alive to their virtues and goodness. Indeed, people seemed to grow more good with one so unselfish and so gentle."

In London, some years later : —

" He was still the same ; time changed him very little. His conversation was as interesting as ever [he was always an excellent relater];

his dark gray eyes still full of varying feeling; his smile half playful, half melancholy, but ever kind. All that was mean, or envious, or harsh, he seemed to turn from so completely that, when with him, it seemed that such things were not. All gentle and tender affections, Nature in her sweetest or grandest moods, pervaded his whole imagination, and left no place for low or evil thoughts; and when in good spirits, his humor, his droll descriptions, and his fun would make the gravest or the saddest laugh."

As to Irving's "state of mind" in Dresden, it is pertinent to quote a passage from what we gather to be a journal kept by Miss Flora Foster : —

"He has written. He has confessed to my mother, as to a true and dear friend, his love for E——, and his conviction of its utter hopelessness. He feels himself unable to combat it. He thinks he must try, by absence, to bring more peace to his mind. Yet he cannot bear to give up our friendship, — an intercourse become so dear to him, and so necessary to his daily happiness. Poor Irving !"

It is well for our peace of mind that we do not know what is going down concerning us in "journals." On his way to the

Herrnhuthers, Mr. Irving wrote to Mrs. Foster : —

" When I consider how I have trifled with my time, suffered painful vicissitudes of feeling, which for a time damaged both mind and body, — when I consider all this, I reproach myself that I did not listen to the first impulse of my mind, and abandon Dresden long since. And yet I think of returning ! Why should I come back to Dresden ? The very inclination that dooms me thither should furnish reasons for my staying away."

In this mood, the Herrnhuthers, in their right-angled, whitewashed world, were little attractive.

" If the Herrnhuthers were right in their notions, the world would have been laid out in squares and angles and right lines, and everything would have been white and black and snuff-color, as they have been clipped by these merciless retrenchers of beauty and enjoyment. And then their dormitories ! Think of between one and two hundred of these simple gentlemen cooped up at night in one great chamber ! What a concert of barrel-organs in this great resounding saloon ! And then their plan of marriage ! The very birds of the air choose their mates from preference and inclination; but this detestable system of *lot!* The sentiment of love may be, and is, in a great measure, a fostered growth of poetry and romance, and balderdashed with false sentiment; but with all its vitiations, it is the beauty and the charm, the flavor and the fragrance, of all intercourse between man and woman; it is the rosy cloud in the morning of life; and if it does too often resolve itself into the shower, yet, to my mind, it only makes our nature more fruitful in what is excellent and amiable."

Better suited him Prague, which is certainly a part of the " naughty world " that Irving preferred : —

"Old Prague still keeps up its warrior look, and swaggers about with its rusty corselet and helm, though both sadly battered. There seems to me to be an air of style and fashion about the first people of Prague, and a good deal of beauty in the fashionable circle. This, perhaps, is owing to my contemplating it from a distance, and my imagination lending it tints occasionally. Both actors and audience, contemplated from the pit of a theatre, look better than when seen in the boxes and behind the scenes. I like to contemplate society in this way occasionally, and to dress it up by the help of fancy, to my own taste. When I get in the midst of it, it is too apt to lose its charm, and then there is the trouble and *ennui* of being obliged to take an active part in the farce; but to be a mere spectator is amusing. I am glad, therefore, that I brought no letters to Prague. I shall leave it with a favorable idea of its society and manners, from knowing nothing accurate of either; and with a firm belief that every pretty woman I have seen is an angel, as I am apt to think every pretty woman, until I have found her out."

In July, 1823, Irving returned to Paris, to the society of the Moores and the fascinations of the gay town, and to fitful literary work. Our author wrote with great facility and rapidity when the inspiration was on him, and produced an astonishing amount of manuscript in a short period; but he often waited and fretted through barren weeks and months for the movement of his fitful genius. His mind was teeming constantly with new projects, and nothing could exceed his industry when once he had taken a work in hand; but he never acquired the exact methodical habits which enable some literary men to calculate their power and quantity of production as accurately as that of a cotton mill.

The political changes in France during

the period of Irving's long sojourn in Paris
do not seem to have taken much of his attention.   In a letter dated October 5, 1824,
he says : " We have had much bustle in
Paris of late, between the death of one king
and the succession of another.   I have become a little callous to public sights, but
have, notwithstanding, been to see the funeral of the late king, and the entrance into
Paris of the present one.   Charles X. begins his reign in a very conciliating manner,
and is really popular.   The Bourbons have
gained great accession of power within a few
years."

The succession of Charles X. was also observed by another foreigner, who was making agreeable personal notes at that time in
Paris, but who is not referred to by Irving,
who for some unexplained reason failed to
meet the genial Scotsman at breakfast.   Perhaps it is to his failure to do so that he owes
the semi-respectful reference to himself in
Carlyle's " Reminiscences."   Lacking the
stimulus to his vocabulary of personal acquaintance, Carlyle simply wrote : " Washington Irving was said to be in Paris, a kind
of lion at that time, whose books I some-

what esteemed. One day the Emerson-
Tennant people bragged that they had engaged him to breakfast with us at a certain
café next morning. We all attended duly,
Strackey among the rest, but no Washington came. 'Couldn't rightly come,' said
Malcolm to me in a judicious *aside*, as we
cheerfully breakfasted without him. I never
saw Washington at all, but still have a mild
esteem of the good man." This ought to be
accepted as evidence of Carlyle's disinclination to say ill-natured things of those he did
not know.

The "Tales of a Traveller" appeared in
1824. In the author's opinion, with which
the best critics agreed, it contained some of
his best writing. He himself said in a letter
to Brevoort, "There was more of an artistic
touch about it, though this is not a thing
to be appreciated by the many." It was
rapidly written. The movement has a delightful spontaneity, and it is wanting in
none of the charms of his style, unless, perhaps, the style is over-refined; but it was not
a novelty, and the public began to criticise
and demand a new note. This may have
been one reason why he turned to a fresh

field and to graver themes. For a time he busied himself on some American essays of a semi-political nature, which were never finished, and he seriously contemplated a Life of Washington; but all these projects were thrown aside for one that kindled his imagination, — the Life of Columbus; and in February, 1826, he was domiciled at Madrid, and settled down to a long period of unremitting and intense labor,

CHAPTER VII.

IN SPAIN.

IRVING'S residence in Spain, which was prolonged till September, 1829, was the most fruitful period in his life, and of considerable consequence to literature. It is not easy to overestimate the debt of Americans to the man who first opened to them the fascinating domain of early Spanish history and romance. We can conceive of it by reflecting upon the blank that would exist without "The Alhambra," "The Conquest of Granada," "The Legends of the Conquest of Spain," and I may add the popular loss if we had not "The Lives of Columbus and his Companions." Irving had the creative touch, or at least the magic of the pen, to give a definite, universal, and romantic interest to whatever he described. We cannot deny him that. A few lines about the inn of the Red Horse at Stratford-on-Avon created a new object of pilgrimage right in the presence of the house and tomb of the poet. And how much of the romantic interest of all the English-reading world in the Alhambra is due to him; the name invariably recalls his own, and every visitor there is conscious of his presence. He has again and again been criticised almost out of court, and written down to the rank of the mere idle humorist; but as often as I take up " The Conquest of Granada " or " The Alhambra " I am aware of something that has eluded the critical analysis, and I conclude that if one cannot write for the few it may be worth while to write for the many.

It was Irving's intention, when he went to Madrid, merely to make a translation of some historical documents which were then appearing, edited by M. Navarrete, from the papers of Bishop Las Casas and the journals of Columbus, entitled " The Voyages of Columbus." But when he found that this publication, although it contained many documents, hitherto unknown, that threw much light on the discovery of the New World, was rather a rich mass of materials for a history than a history itself, and that he had access in Madrid libraries to great collections of Spanish colonial history, he changed his plan, and determined to write a Life of Columbus. His studies for this led him deep into the old chronicles and legends of Spain, and out of these, with his own travel and observation, came those books of mingled fables, sentiment, fact, and humor which are after all the most enduring fruits of his residence in Spain.

Notwithstanding his absorption in literary pursuits, Irving was not denied the charm of domestic society, which was all his life his chief delight. The house he most frequented in Madrid was that of Mr. D'Oubril, the Russian Minister. In his charming household were Madame D'Oubril and her niece, Mademoiselle Antoinette Bollviller, and Prince Dolgorouki, a young *attaché* of the legation. His letters to Prince Dolgorouki and to Mademoiselle Antoinette give a most lively and entertaining picture of his residence and travels in Spain. In one of them to the prince, who was temporarily absent from the city, we have glimpses of the happy hours, the happiest of all hours, passed in this refined family circle. Here is one that exhibits the still fresh romance in the heart of forty-four years : —

" Last evening, at your house, we had one of the most lovely tableaux I ever beheld. It was the conception of Murillo, represented by Madame A———. Mademoiselle Antoinette arranged the tableau with her usual good taste, and the effect was enchanting. It was more like a vision of something spiritual and celestial than a representation of anything merely mortal ; or rather it was woman as in my romantic days I have been apt to imagine her, approaching to the angelic nature. I have frequently admired Madame A——— as a mere beautiful woman, when I have seen her dressed up in the fantastic attire of the *mode ;* but here I beheld her elevated into a representative of the divine purity and grace, exceeding even the *beau idéal* of the painter, for she even surpassed in beauty the picture of Murillo. I felt as if I could have knelt down and worshiped her. Heavens! what power women would have over us, if they knew how to sustain the attractions which nature has bestowed upon them, and which we are so ready to assist by our imaginations ! For my part, I am superstitious in my admiration of them, and like to walk in a perpetual delusion, decking them out as divinities. I thank no one to undeceive me, and to prove that they are mere mortals."

And he continues in another strain: —

"How full of interest everything is connected with the old times in Spain! I am more and more delighted with the old literature of the country, its chronicles, plays, and romances. It has the wild vigor and luxuriance of the forests of my native country, which, however savage and entangled, are more captivating to my imagination than the finest parks and cultivated woodlands.

"As I live in the neighborhood of the library of the Jesuits' College of St. Isidoro, I pass most of my mornings there. You cannot think what a delight I feel in passing through its galleries, filled with old parchment-bound books. It is a perfect wilderness of curiosity to me. What a deep-felt, quiet luxury there is in delving into the rich ore of these old, neglected volumes! How these hours of uninterrupted intellectual enjoyment, so tranquil and independent, repay one for the *ennui* and disappointment too often experienced in the intercourse of society! How they serve to bring back the feelings into a harmonious tone, after being jarred and put out of tune by the collisions with the world!"

With the romantic period of Spanish his-

tory Irving was in ardent sympathy. The
story of the Saracens entranced his mind;
his imagination disclosed its Oriental quality while he pored over the romance and
the ruin of that land of fierce contrasts,
of arid wastes beaten by the burning sun,
valleys blooming with intoxicating beauty,
cities of architectural splendor and picturesque squalor. It is matter of regret that
he, who seemed to need the southern sun to
ripen his genius, never made a pilgrimage
into the East, and gave to the world pictures
of the lands that he would have touched
with the charm of their own color and the
witchery of their own romance.

I will quote again from the letters, for
they reveal the man quite as well as the
more formal and better known writings.
His first sight of the Alhambra is given in
a letter to Mademoiselle Bollviller : —

"Our journey through La Mancha was cold
and uninteresting, excepting when we passed
through the scenes of some of the exploits of
Don Quixote. We were repaid, however, by a
night amidst the scenery of the Sierra Morena,
seen by the light of the full moon. I do not
know how this scenery would appear in the day-

time, but by moonlight it is wonderfully wild and
romantic, especially after passing the summit of
the Sierra. As the day dawned we entered the
stern and savage defiles of the Despeña Perros,
which equals the wild landscapes of Salvator
Rosa. For some time we continued winding
along the brinks of precipices, overhung with
cragged and fantastic rocks; and after a succession of such rude and sterile scenes we swept
down to Carolina, and found ourselves in another climate. The orange-trees, the aloes, and
myrtle began to make their appearance; we felt
the warm temperature of the sweet South, and
began to breathe the balmy air of Andalusia. At
Andujar we were delighted with the neatness
and cleanliness of the houses, the *patios* planted
with orange and citron trees, and refreshed by
fountains. We passed a charming evening on the
banks of the famous Guadalquivir, enjoying the
mild, balmy air of a southern evening, and rejoicing in the certainty that we were at length in
this land of promise. . . .

"But Granada, *bellissima* Granada! Think what
must have been our delight when, after passing
the famous bridge of Pinos, the scene of many a
bloody encounter between Moor and Christian,
and remarkable for having been the place where
Columbus was overtaken by the messenger of
Isabella, when about to abandon Spain in de-

spair, we turned a promontory of the arid mountains of Elvira, and Granada, with its towers, its Alhambra, and its snowy mountains, burst upon our sight! The evening sun shone gloriously upon its red towers as we approached it, and gave a mellow tone to the rich scenery of the vega. It was like the magic glow which poetry and romance have shed over this enchanting place. . . .

"The more I contemplate these places, the more my admiration is awakened for the elegant habits and delicate taste of the Moorish monarchs. The delicately ornamented walls; the aromatic groves, mingling with the freshness and the enlivening sounds of fountains and rivers of water; the retired baths, bespeaking purity and refinement; the balconies and galleries, open to the fresh mountain breeze, and overlooking the loveliest scenery of the valley of the Darro and the magnificent expanse of the vega, — it is impossible to contemplate this delicious abode and not feel an admiration of the genius and the poetical spirit of those who first devised this earthly paradise. There is an intoxication of heart and soul in looking over such scenery at this genial season. All nature is just teeming with new life, and putting on the first delicate verdure and bloom of spring. The almond - trees are in blossom; the fig-trees are beginning to sprout;

everything is in the tender bud, the young leaf, or the half-open flower. The beauty of the season is but half developed, so that while there is enough to yield present delight there is the flattering promise of still further enjoyment. Good heavens! after passing two years amidst the sunburnt wastes of Castile, to be let loose to rove at large over this fragrant and lovely land!"

It was not easy, however, even in the Alhambra, perfectly to call up the past : —

"The verity of the present checks and chills the imagination in its picturings of the past. I have been trying to conjure up images of Boabdil passing in regal splendor through these courts; of his beautiful queen; of the Abencerrages, the Gomares, and the other Moorish cavaliers, who once filled these halls with the glitter of arms and the splendor of Oriental luxury; but I am continually awakened from my reveries by the jargon of an Andalusian peasant who is setting out rose-bushes, and the song of a pretty Andalusian girl who shows the Alhambra, and who is chanting a little romance that has probably been handed down from generation to generation since the time of the Moors."

In another letter, written from Seville, he returns to the subject of the Moors.

He is describing an excursion to Alcala de la Guadayra :—

"Nothing can be more charming than the windings of the little river among banks hanging with gardens and orchards of all kinds of delicate southern fruits, and tufted with flowers and aromatic plants. The nightingales throng this lovely little valley as numerously as they do the gardens of Aranjuez. Every bend of the river presents a new landscape, for it is beset by old Moorish mills of the most picturesque forms, each mill having an embattled tower, — a memento of the valiant tenure by which those gallant fellows, the Moors, held this earthly paradise, having to be ready at all times for war, and as it were to work with one hand and fight with the other. It is impossible to travel about Andalusia and not imbibe a kind feeling for those Moors. They deserved this beautiful country. They won it bravely ; they enjoyed it generously and kindly. No lover ever delighted more to cherish and adorn a mistress, to heighten and illustrate her charms, and to vindicate and defend her against all the world than did the Moors to embellish, enrich, elevate, and defend their beloved Spain. Everywhere I meet traces of their sagacity, courage, urbanity, high poetical feeling, and elegant taste. The noblest institu-

tions in this part of Spain, the best inventions
for comfortable and agreeable living, and all
those habitudes and customs which throw a peculiar and Oriental charm over the Andalusian
mode of living may be traced to the Moors.
Whenever I enter these beautiful marble *patios*,
set out with shrubs and flowers, refreshed by
fountains, sheltered with awnings from the sun;
where the air is cool at noonday, the ear delighted in sultry summer by the sound of falling
water; where, in a word, a little paradise is shut
up within the walls of home, I think on the poor
Moors, the inventors of all these delights. I am
at times almost ready to join in sentiment with
a worthy friend and countryman of mine whom
I met in Malaga, who swears the Moors are the
only people that ever deserved the country, and
prays to Heaven that they may come over from
Africa and conquer it again."

In a following paragraph we get a glimpse
of a world, however, that the author loves
still more : —

"Tell me everything about the children. I
suppose the discreet princess will soon consider
it an indignity to be ranked among the number. I am told she is growing with might and
main, and is determined not to stop until she is a
woman outright. I would give all the money

in my pocket to be with those dear little women
at the round table in the saloon, or on the grass-
plot in the garden, to tell them some marvelous
tales."

And again : —

" Give my love to all my dear little friends
of the round table, from the discreet princess
down to the little blue-eyed boy.   Tell *la pe-
tite Marie* that I still remain true to her, though
surrounded by all the beauties of Seville; and
that I swear (but this she must keep between
ourselves) that there is not a little woman to
compare with her in all Andalusia."

The publication of " The Life of Columbus," which had been delayed by Irving's
anxiety to secure historical accuracy in every
detail, did not take place till February, 1828.
For the English copyright Mr. Murray paid
him £3,150.   He wrote an abridgment of
it, which he presented to his generous publisher, and which was a very profitable book
(the first edition of ten thousand copies sold
immediately).   This was followed by the
" Companions," and by " The Chronicle of
the Conquest of Granada," for which he received two thousand guineas.   " The Alhambra " was not published till just before

Irving's return to America, in 1832, and was brought out by Mr. Bentley, who bought it for one thousand guineas.

"The Conquest of Granada," which I am told Irving in his latter years regarded as the best of all his works, was declared by Coleridge "a *chef-d'œuvre* of its kind." I think it bears re-reading as well as any of the Spanish books. Of the reception of the "Columbus" the author was very doubtful. Before it was finished he wrote: —

"I have lost confidence in the favorable disposition of my countrymen, and look forward to cold scrutiny and stern criticism, and this is a line of writing in which I have not hitherto ascertained my own powers. Could I afford it, I should like to write, and to lay my writings aside when finished. There is an independent delight in study and in the creative exercise of the pen; we live in a world of dreams, but publication lets in the noisy rabble of the world, and there is an end of our dreaming."

In a letter to Brevoort, February, 23, 1828, he fears that he can never regain

"That delightful confidence which I once enjoyed of not the good opinion, but the good will, of my countrymen. To me it is always ten times more gratifying to be liked than to be admired; and I confess to you, though I am a little too proud to confess it to the world, the idea that the kindness of my countrymen toward me was withering caused me for a long time the most weary depression of spirits, and disheartened me from making any literary exertions."

It has been a popular notion that Irving's career was uniformly one of ease. In this same letter he exclaims: "With all my exertions, I seem always to keep about up to my chin in troubled water, while the world, I suppose, thinks I am sailing smoothly, with wind and tide in my favor."

In a subsequent letter to Brevoort, dated at Seville, December 26, 1828, occurs almost the only piece of impatience and sarcasm that this long correspondence affords. "Columbus" had succeeded beyond his expectation, and its popularity was so great that some enterprising American had projected an abridgment, which it seems would not be protected by the copyright of the original. Irving writes: —

"I have just sent to my brother an abridgment of 'Columbus' to be published immediately, as I find some paltry fellow is pirating an abridgment. Thus every line of life has its depredation. 'There be land rats and water rats, land pirates and water pirates, — I mean thieves,' as old Shylock says. I feel vexed at this shabby attempt to purloin this work from me, it having really cost me more toil and trouble than all my other productions, and being one that I trusted would keep me current with my countrymen; but we are making rapid advances in literature in America, and have already attained many of the literary vices and diseases of the old countries of Europe. We swarm with reviewers, though we have scarce original works sufficient for them to alight and prey upon, and we closely imitate all the worst tricks of the trade and of the craft in England. Our literature, before long, will be like some of those premature and aspiring whipsters, who become old men before they are young ones, and fancy they prove their manhood by their profligacy and their diseases."

But the work had an immediate, continued, and deserved success. It was critically contrasted with Robertson's account of Columbus, and it is open to the charge of too much rhetorical color here and there, and it is at times too diffuse; but its substantial accuracy is not questioned, and the glow of the narrative springs legitimately from the romance of the theme. Irving understood, what our later historians have fully appreciated, the advantage of vivid individual portraiture in historical narrative. His conception of the character and mission of Columbus is largely outlined, but firmly and most carefully executed, and is one of the noblest in literature. I cannot think it idealized, though it required a poetic sensibility to enter into sympathy with the magnificent dreamer, who was regarded by his own generation as the fool of an idea. A more prosaic treatment would have utterly failed to represent that mind, which existed from boyhood in an ideal world, and, amid frustrated hopes, shattered plans, and ignoble returns for his sacrifices, could always rebuild its glowing projects, and conquer obloquy and death itself with immortal anticipations.

Towards the close of his residence in Spain, Irving received unexpectedly the appointment of Secretary of Legation to the Court of St. James, at which Louis McLane was American Minister; and after some hesitation, and upon the urgency of his friends, he accepted it. He was in the thick of literary projects. One of these was the History of the Conquest of Mexico, which he afterwards surrendered to Mr. Prescott and another was the " Life of Washington," which was to wait many years for fulfillment. His natural diffidence and his reluctance to a routine life made him shrink from the diplomatic appointment; but once engaged in it, and launched again in London society, he was reconciled to the situation. Of honors there was no lack, nor of the adulation of social and literary circles. In April, 1830, the Royal Society of Literature awarded him one of the two annual gold medals placed at the disposal of the society by George IV., to be given to authors of literary works of eminent merit, the other being voted to the historian Hallam; and this distinction was followed by the degree of D. C. L. from the University of Oxford, — a title which the modest author never used.

CHAPTER VIII.

In 1831 Mr. Irving was thrown, by his
diplomatic position, into the thick of the
political and social tumult, when the Reform Bill was pending and war was expected in Europe. It is interesting to note
that for a time he laid aside his attitude of
the dispassionate observer, and caught the
general excitement. He writes in March,
expecting that the fate of the cabinet will
be determined in a week, looking daily for
decisive news from Paris, and fearing dismal tidings from Poland. "However," he
goes on to say in a vague way, "the great
cause of all the world will go on. What a
stirring moment it is to live in! I never
took such intense interest in newspapers.
It seems to me as if life were breaking out
anew with me, or that I were entering upon
quite a new and almost unknown career of

existence, and I rejoice to find my sensibili-
ties, which were waning as to many objects
of past interest, reviving with all their
freshness and vivacity at the scenes and
prospects opening around me." He expects
the breaking of the thralldom of falsehood
woven over the human mind; and, more
definitely, hopes that the Reform Bill will
prevail. Yet he is oppressed by the gloom
hanging over the booksellers' trade, which
he thinks will continue until reform and chol-
era have passed away.

During the last months of his residence in
England, the author renewed his impressions of Stratford (the grateful landlady of
the Red Horse Inn showed him a poker
which was locked up among the treasures of
her house, on which she had caused to be
engraved " Geoffrey Crayon's Sceptre ") ;
spent some time at Newstead Abbey ; and
had the sorrowful pleasure in London of seeing Scott once more, and for the last time.
The great novelist, in the sad eclipse of his
powers, was staying in the city, on his way
to Italy, and Mr. Lockhart asked Irving to
dine with him. It was but a melancholy
repast. " Ah," said Scott, as Irving gave

him his arm, after dinner, " the times are changed, my good fellow, since we went over the Eildon Hills together. It is all nonsense to tell a man that his mind is not affected when his body is in this state."

Irving retired from the legation in September, 1831, to return home, the longing to see his native land having become intense; but his arrival in New York was delayed till May, 1832.

If he had any doubts of the sentiments of his countrymen toward him, his reception in New York dissipated them. America greeted her most famous literary man with a spontaneous outburst of love and admiration. The public banquet in New York, that was long remembered for its brilliancy, was followed by the tender of the same tribute in other cities, — an honor which his unconquerable shrinking from this kind of publicity compelled him to decline. The "Dutch Herodotus, Diedrich Knickerbocker," to use the phrase of a toast, having come out of one such encounter with fair credit, did not care to tempt Providence further. The thought of making a dinner-table speech threw him into a sort of whimsical

panic,— a noble infirmity, which characterized also Hawthorne and Thackeray.

The enthusiasm manifested for the home-
sick author was equaled by his own for the
land and the people he supremely loved.
Nor was his surprise at the progress made
during seventeen years less than his delight
in it. His native place had become a city
of two hundred thousand inhabitants; the
accumulation of wealth and the activity of
trade astonished him, and the literary stir
was scarcely less unexpected. The steamboat had come to be used, so that he seemed
to be transported from place to place by
magic; and on a near view the politics of
America seemed not less interesting than
those of Europe. The nullification battle
was set; the currency conflict still raged;
it was a time of inflation and land speculation; the West, every day more explored
and opened, was the land of promise for
capital and energy. Fortunes were made
in a day by buying lots in " paper towns."
Into some of these speculations Irving put
his savings; the investments were as permanent as they were unremunerative.

Irving's first desire, however, on his re-

11

covery from the state of astonishment into which these changes plunged him, was to make himself thoroughly acquainted with the entire country and its development. To this end he made an extended tour in the South and West, which passed beyond the bounds of frontier settlement. The fruit of his excursion into the Pawnee country, on the waters of the Arkansas, a region untraversed by white men, except solitary trappers, was " A Tour on the Prairies," a sort of romance of reality, which remains to-day as good a description as we have of hunting adventure on the plains. It led also to the composition of other books on the West, which were more or less mere pieces of book-making for the market.

Our author was far from idle. Indeed, he could not afford to be. Although he had received considerable sums from his books, and perhaps enough for his own simple wants, the responsibility of the support of his two brothers, Peter and Ebenezer, and several nieces, devolved upon him. And, besides, he had a longing to make himself a home, where he could pursue his calling undisturbed, and indulge the sweets of domestic and rural life, which of all things lay nearest his heart. And these two undertakings compelled him to be diligent with his pen to the end of his life. The spot he chose for his " Roost" was a little farm on the bank of the river at Tarrytown, close to his old Sleepy Hollow haunt, one of the loveliest, if not the most picturesque, situations on the Hudson. At first he intended nothing more than a summer retreat, inexpensive and simply furnished. But his experience was that of all who buy, and renovate, and build. The farm had on it a small stone Dutch cottage, built about a century before, and inhabited by one of the Van Tassels. This was enlarged, still preserving the quaint Dutch characteristics ; it acquired a tower and a whimsical weathercock, the delight of the owner (" it was brought from Holland by Gill Davis, the King of Coney Island, who says he got it from a windmill which they were demolishing at the gate of Rotterdam, which windmill has been mentioned in ' Knickerbocker ' "), and became one of the most snug and picturesque residences on the river. When the slip of Melrose ivy, which was

brought over from Scotland by Mrs. Renwick and given to the author, had grown
and well overrun it, the house, in the midst
of sheltering groves and secluded walks, was
as pretty a retreat as a poet could desire.
But the little nook proved to have an insa-
tiable capacity for swallowing up money, as
the necessities of the author's establishment
increased : there was always something to
be done to the grounds ; some alterations in
the house ; a green-house, a stable, a gar-
dener's cottage, to be built, — and to the
very end the outlay continued.   The cottage
necessitated economy in other personal ex-
penses, and incessant employment of his pen.
But Sunnyside, as the place was named, became the dearest spot on earth to him ; it
was his residence, from which he tore himself
with reluctance, and to which he returned
with eager longing ; and here, surrounded by
relatives whom he loved, he passed nearly all
the remainder of his years, in as happy conditions, I think, as a bachelor ever enjoyed.
His intellectual activity was unremitting,
he had no lack of friends, there was only
now and then a discordant note in the general estimation of his literary work, and he

was the object of the most tender care from his nieces. Already, he writes, in October, 1838, " my little cottage is well stocked. I have Ebenezer's five girls, and himself also, whenever he can be spared from town; sister Catherine and her daughter; Mr. Davis occasionally, with casual visits from all the rest of our family connection. The cottage, therefore, is never lonely." I like to dwell in thought upon this happy home, a real haven of rest after many wanderings; a seclusion broken only now and then by enforced absence, like that in Madrid as minister, but enlivened by many welcome guests. Perhaps the most notorious of these was a young Frenchman, a "somewhat quiet guest," who, after several months' imprisonment on board a French man-of-war, was set on shore at Norfolk, and spent a couple of months in New York and its vicinity, in 1837. This visit was vividly recalled to Irving in a letter to his sister, Mrs. Storrow, who was in Paris in 1853, and had just been presented at court:—

" Louis Napoleon and Eugénie Montijo, Emperor and Empress of France! one of whom I have had a guest at my cottage on the Hudson;

the other, whom, when a child, I have had on
my knee at Granada. It seems to cap the cli-
max of the strange dramas of which Paris has
been the theatre during my life-time. I have re-
peatedly thought that each grand *coup de théâtre*
would be the last that would occur in my time;
but each has been succeeded by another equally
striking; and what will be the next, who can
conjecture?

"The last time I saw Eugénie Montijo she was
one of the reigning belles of Madrid; and she
and her giddy circle had swept away my charming young friend, the beautiful and accomplished
—— ——, into their career of fashionable dis-
sipation. Now Eugénie is upon a throne, and
—— a voluntary recluse in a convent of one of
the most rigorous orders! Poor ——! Perhaps, however, her fate may ultimately be the
happiest of the two. 'The storm' with her 'is
o'er, and she's at rest;' but the other is launched
upon a returnless shore, on a dangerous sea, in-
famous for its tremendous shipwrecks. Am I to
live to see the catastrophe of her career, and the
end of this suddenly conjured-up empire, which
seems to be of 'such stuff as dreams are made
of'?"

As we have seen, the large sums Irving
earned by his pen were not spent in selfish

indulgence. His habits and tastes were simple, and little would have sufficed for his individual needs. He cared not much for money, and seemed to want it only to increase the happiness of those who were confided to his care. A man less warm-hearted and more selfish, in his circumstances, would have settled down to a life of more ease and less responsibility.

To go back to the period of his return to America. He was now past middle life, having returned to New York in his fiftieth year. But he was in the full flow of literary productiveness. I have noted the dates of his achievements, because his development was somewhat tardy compared with that of many of his contemporaries; but he had the " staying " qualities. The first crop of his mind was of course the most original; time and experience had toned down his exuberant humor; but the spring of his fancy was as free, his vigor was not abated, and his art was more refined. Some of his best work was yet to be done. And it is worthy of passing mention, in regard to his later productions, that his admirable sense of literary proportion, which

is wanting in many good writers, characterized his work to the end.

High as his position was as a man of letters at this time, the consideration in which
he was held was much broader than that, —
it was that of one of the first citizens of the
Republic. His friends, readers, and admirers were not merely the literary class and the
general public, but included nearly all the
prominent statesmen of the time. Almost
any career in public life would have been
open to him if he had lent an ear to their
solicitations. But political life was not to
his taste, and it would have been fatal to his
sensitive spirit. It did not require much
self-denial, perhaps, to decline the candi-
dacy for mayor of New York, or the honor
of standing for Congress; but he put aside
also the distinction of a seat in Mr. Van
Buren's Cabinet as Secretary of the Navy.
His main reason for declining it, aside from
a diffidence in his own judgment in public
matters, was his dislike of the turmoil of
political life in Washington, and his sensi-
tiveness to personal attacks which beset the
occupants of high offices. But he also had
come to a political divergence with Mr.

Van Buren. He liked the man, — he liked almost everybody, — and esteemed him as a friend, but he apprehended trouble from the new direction of the party in power. Irving was almost devoid of party prejudice, and he never seemed to have strongly marked political opinions. Perhaps his nearest confession to a creed is contained in a letter he wrote to a member of the House of Representatives, Gouverneur Kemble, a little time before the offer of a position in the cabinet, in which he said that he did not relish some points of Van Buren's policy, nor believe in the honesty of some of his elbow counselors. I quote a passage from it : —

" As far as I know my own mind, I am thoroughly a republican, and attached, from complete conviction, to the institutions of my country ; but I am a republican without gall, and have no bitterness in my creed. I have no relish for Puritans, either in religion or politics, who are for pushing principles to an extreme, and for overturning everything that stands in the way of their own zealous career. . . . Ours is a government of compromise. We have several great and distinct interests bound up together, which,

if not separately consulted and severally accommodated, may harass and impair each other.
. . . I always distrust the soundness of political
councils that are accompanied by acrimonious
and disparaging attacks upon any great class of
our fellow-citizens. Such are those urged to the
disadvantage of the great trading and financial
classes of our country."

During the ten years preceding his mission to Spain, Irving kept fagging away at
the pen, doing a good deal of miscellaneous
and ephemeral work. Among his other engagements was that of regular contributor
to the "Knickerbocker Magazine," for a salary of two thousand dollars. He wrote the
editor that he had observed that man, as he
advances in life, is subject to a plethora of
the mind, occasioned by an accumulation of
wisdom upon the brain, and that he becomes fond of telling long stories and doling
out advice, to the annoyance of his friends.
To avoid becoming the bore of the domestic circle, he proposed to ease off this sur-
charge of the intellect by inflicting his te-
diousness on the public through the pages of
the periodical. The arrangement brought
reputation to the magazine (which was pub-

lished in the days when the honor of being
in print was supposed by the publisher to
be ample compensation to the scribe), but
little profit to Mr. Irving.   During this
period he interested himself in an international copyright, as a means of fostering our
young literature.   He found that a work of
merit, written by an American who had not
established a commanding name in the market, met very cavalier treatment from our
publishers, who frankly said that they need
not trouble themselves about native works,
when they could pick up every day successful books from the British press, for which
they had to pay no copyright.   Irving's ad-
vocacy of the proposed law was entirely unselfish, for his own market was secure.

His chief works in these ten years were,
" A Tour on the Prairies," " Recollections
of Abbotsford and Newstead Abbey," " The
Legends of the Conquest of Spain," "Asto-
ria " (the heavy part of the work of it
was done by his nephew Pierre), " Captain
Bonneville," and a number of graceful occasional papers, collected afterwards under
the title of " Wolfert's Roost."   Two other
books may properly be mentioned here, al-

though they did not appear until after his return from his absence of four years and a half at the court of Madrid; these are the " Biography of Goldsmith " and " Mahomet and his Successors." At the age of sixty-six, he laid aside the " Life of Washington," on which he was engaged, and rapidly "threw off " these two books. The " Goldsmith " was enlarged from a sketch he had made twenty-five years before. It is an exquisite, sympathetic piece of work, without pretension or any subtle verbal analysis, but on the whole an excellent interpretation of the character. Author and subject had much in common: Irving had at least a kindly sympathy for the vagabondish inclinations of his predecessor, and with his humorous and cheerful regard of the world; perhaps it is significant of a deeper unity in character that both, at times, fancied they could please an intolerant world by attempting to play the flute. The " Mahomet " is a popular narrative, which throws no new light on the subject; it is pervaded by the author's charm of style and equity of judgment, but it lacks the virility of Gibbon's masterly picture of the Arabian prophet and the Saracenic onset.

We need not dwell longer upon this period. One incident of it, however, cannot be passed in silence : that was the abandonment of his life-long project of writing the History of the Conquest of Mexico to Mr. William H. Prescott. It had been a scheme of his boyhood ; he had made collections of materials for it during his first residence in Spain; and he was actually and absorbedly engaged in the composition of the first chapters, when he was sounded by Mr. Cogswell, of the Astor Library, in behalf of Mr. Prescott. Some conversation showed that Mr. Prescott was contemplating the subject upon which Mr. Irving was engaged, and the latter instantly authorized Mr. Cogswell to say that he abandoned it. Although our author was somewhat far advanced, and Mr. Prescott had not yet collected his materials, Irving renounced the glorious theme in such a manner that Prescott never suspected the pain and loss it cost him, nor the full extent of his own obligation. Some years afterwards Irving wrote to his nephew that in giving it up he in a manner gave up his bread, as he had no other subject to supply its place : " I was," he wrote, " dismounted from my *cheval de bataille,* and have never been completely mounted since." But he added that he was not sorry for the warm impulse that induced him to abandon the subject, and that Mr. Prescott's treatment of it had justified his opinion of him. Notwithstanding Prescott's very brilliant work, we cannot but feel some regret that Irving did not write a Conquest of Mexico. His method, as he outlined it, would have been the natural one. Instead of partially satisfying the reader's curiosity in a preliminary essay, in which the Aztec civilization was exposed, Irving would have begun with the entry of the conquerors, and carried his reader step by step onward, letting him share all the excitement and surprise of discovery which the invaders experienced, and learn of the wonders of the country in the manner most likely to impress both the imagination and the memory; and with his artistic sense of the value of the picturesque he would have brought into strong relief the *dramatis personæ* of the story.

In 1842, Irving was tendered the honor of the mission to Madrid. It was an entire surprise to himself and to his friends. He came to look upon this as the "crowning honor of his life," and yet when the news first reached him he paced up and down his room, excited and astonished, revolving in his mind the separation from home and friends, and was heard murmuring, half to himself and half to his nephew, "It is hard, —very hard; yet I must try to bear it. God tempers the wind to the shorn lamb." His acceptance of the position was doubtless influenced by the intended honor to his profession, by the gratifying manner in which it came to him, by his desire to please his friends, and the belief, which was a delusion, that diplomatic life in Madrid would offer no serious interruption to his "Life of Washington," in which he had just become engaged. The nomination, the suggestion of Daniel Webster, Tyler's Secretary of State, was cordially approved by the President and cabinet, and confirmed almost by acclamation in the Senate. "Ah," said Mr. Clay, who was opposing nearly all the President's appointments, "this is a nomination everybody will concur in!" "If a person of more merit and higher qualification," wrote Mr. Webster in his official no-

tification, " had presented himself, great as
is my personal regard for you, I should have
yielded it to higher considerations." No
other appointment could have been made so
complimentary to Spain, and it remains to
this day one of the most honorable to his
own country.

In reading Irving's letters written during
his third visit abroad, you are conscious
that the glamour of life is gone for him,
though not his kindliness towards the world,
and that he is subject to few illusions; the
show and pageantry no longer enchant, —
they only weary. The novelty was gone,
and he was no longer curious to see great
sights and great people. He had declined a
public dinner in New York, and he put aside
the same hospitality offered by Liverpool
and by Glasgow. In London he attended
the Queen's grand fancy ball, which surpassed anything he had seen in splendor
and picturesque effect. " The personage,"
he writes, " who appeared least to enjoy the
scene seemed to me to be the little Queen
herself. She was flushed and heated, and
evidently fatigued and oppressed with the
state she had to keep up and the regal robes

in which she was arrayed, and especially by
a crown of gold, which weighed heavy on
her brow, and to which she was continually
raising her hand to move it slightly when it
pressed. I hope and trust her real crown
sits easier." The bearing of Prince Albert
he found prepossessing, and he adds, " He
speaks English very well;" as if that were a
useful accomplishment for an English Prince
Consort. His reception at court and by
the ministers and diplomatic corps was very
kind, and he greatly enjoyed meeting his
old friends, Leslie, Rogers, and Moore. At
Paris, in an informal presentation to the
royal family, he experienced a very cordial
welcome from the King and Queen and
Madame Adelaide, each of whom took occasion to say something complimentary about
his writings; but he escaped as soon as possible from social engagements. "Amidst
all the splendors of London and Paris, I find
my imagination refuses to take fire, and my
heart still yearns after dear little Sunnyside." Of an anxious friend in Paris, who
thought Irving was ruining his prospects by
neglecting to leave his card with this or
that duchess who had sought his acquaint-

12

ance, he writes : " He attributes all this to very excessive modesty, not dreaming that the empty intercourse of saloons with people of rank and fashion could be a bore to one who has run the rounds of society for the greater part of half a century, and who likes to consult his own humor and pursuits."

When Irving reached Madrid the affairs of the kingdom had assumed a powerful dramatic interest, wanting in none of the romantic elements that characterize the whole history of the peninsula. " The future career [he writes] of this gallant soldier, Espartero, whose merits and services have placed him at the head of the government, and the future fortunes of these isolated little princesses, the Queen and her sister, have an uncertainty hanging about them worthy of the fifth act in a melodrama." The drama continued, with constant shifting of scene, as long as Irving remained in Spain, and gave to his diplomatic life intense interest, and at times perilous excitement. His letters are full of animated pictures of the changing progress of the play ; and although they belong rather to the gossip of history than to literary biography, they cannot be altogether omitted. The duties which the minister had to perform were unusual, delicate, and difficult; but I believe he acquitted himself of them with the skill of a born diplomatist. When he went to Spain before, in 1826, Ferdinand VII. was, by aid of French troops, on the throne, the liberties of the kingdom were crushed, and her most enlightened men were in exile. While he still resided there, in 1829, Ferdinand married, for his fourth wife, Maria Christina, sister of the King of Naples, and niece of the Queen of Louis Philippe. By her he had two daughters, his only children. In order that his own progeny might succeed him, he set aside the Salique law (which had been imposed by France) just before his death, in 1833, and revived the old Spanish law of succession. His eldest daughter, then three years old, was proclaimed Queen, by the name of Isabella II., and her mother guardian during her minority, which would end at the age of fourteen. Don Carlos, the king's eldest brother, immediately set up the standard of rebellion, supported by the absolutist aristocracy, the monks, and a great part of the clergy. The

liberals rallied to the Queen. The Queen
Regent did not, however, act in good faith
with the popular party: she resisted all
salutary reform, would not restore the Constitution of 1812 until compelled to by a
popular uprising, and disgraced herself by
a scandalous connection with one Muños,
one of the royal body guards. She enriched
this favorite and amassed a vast fortune for
herself, which she sent out of the country.
In 1839, when Don Carlos was driven out
of the country by the patriot soldier Espartero, she endeavored to gain him over to
her side, but failed. Espartero became Regent, and Maria Christina repaired to Paris,
where she was received with great distinction by Louis Philippe, and Paris became
the focus of all sorts of machinations against
the constitutional government of Spain, and
of plots for its overthrow. One of these
had just been defeated at the time of Irving's arrival. It was a desperate attempt
of a band of soldiers of the rebel army to
carry off the little Queen and her sister,
which was frustrated only by the gallant
resistance of the halberdiers in the palace.
The little princesses had scarcely recovered

from the horror of this night attack when our minister presented his credentials to the Queen through the Regent, thus breaking a diplomatic dead-lock, in which he was followed by all the other embassies except the French. I take some passages from the author's description of his first audience at the royal palace : —

"We passed through the spacious court, up the noble staircase, and through the long suites of apartments of this splendid edifice, most of them silent and vacant, the casements closed to keep out the heat, so that a twilight reigned throughout the mighty pile, not a little emblematical of the dubious fortunes of its inmates. It seemed more like traversing a convent than a palace. I ought to have mentioned that in ascending the grand staircase we found the portal at the head of it, opening into the royal suite of apartments, still bearing the marks of the midnight attack upon the palace in October last, when an attempt was made to get possession of the persons of the little Queen and her sister, to carry them off. . . . The marble casements of the doors had been shattered in several places, and the double doors themselves pierced all over with bullet holes, from the musketry that played upon them from the staircase during that eventful night. What must have been the feelings of those poor children, on listening, from their apartment, to the horrid tumult, the outcries of a furious multitude, and the reports of fire-arms echoing and reverberating through the vaulted halls and spacious courts of this immense edifice, and dubious whether their own lives were not the object of the assault!

" After passing through various chambers of the palace, now silent and sombre, but which I had traversed in former days, on grand court occasions in the time of Ferdinand VII., when they were glittering with all the splendor of a court, we paused in a great saloon, with high-vaulted ceiling incrusted with florid devices in porcelain, and hung with silken tapestry, but all in dim twilight, like the rest of the palace. At one end of the saloon the door opened to an almost interminable range of other chambers, through which, at a distance, we had a glimpse of some indistinct figures in black. They glided into the saloon slowly, and with noiseless steps. It was the little Queen, with her governess, Madame Mina, widow of the general of that name, and her guardian, the excellent Arguelles, all in deep mourning for the Duke of Orleans. The little Queen advanced some steps within the saloon and then paused. Madame Mina took her station a little distance behind her. The Count Almo-

dovar then introduced me to the Queen in my
official capacity, and she received me with a
grave and quiet welcome, expressed in a very
low voice. She is nearly twelve years of age,
and is sufficiently well grown for her years. She
had a somewhat fair complexion, quite pale, with
bluish or light gray eyes; a grave demeanor,
but a graceful deportment. I could not but regard her with deep interest, knowing what important concerns depended upon the life of this
fragile little being, and to what a stormy and
precarious career she might be destined. Her
solitary position, also, separated from all her
kindred except her little sister, a mere effigy of
royalty in the hands of statesmen, and surrounded
by the formalities and ceremonials of state,
which spread sterility around the occupant of a
throne."

I have quoted this passage not more on
account of its intrinsic interest, than as a
specimen of the author's consummate art of
conveying an impression by what I may call
the tone of his style; and this appears in
all his correspondence relating to this picturesque and eventful period. During the
four years of his residence the country was
in a constant state of excitement and often
of panic. Armies were marching over the

kingdom. Madrid was in a state of siege, expecting an assault at one time; confusion reigned amid the changing adherents about the person of the child Queen. The duties of a minister were perplexing enough, when the Spanish government was changing its character and its *personnel* with the rapidity of shifting scenes in a pantomime. "This consumption of ministers," wrote Irving to Mr. Webster, "is appalling. To carry on a negotiation with such transient functionaries is like bargaining at the window of a railroad car: before you can get a reply to a proposition the other party is out of sight."

Apart from politics, Irving's residence was full of half-melancholy recollections and associations. In a letter to his old comrade Prince Dolgorouki, then Russian Minister at Naples, he recalls the days of their delightful intercourse at the D'Oubrils: —

"Time dispels charms and illusions. You remember how much I was struck with a beautiful young woman (1 will not mention names) who appeared in a tableau as Murillo's Virgin of the Assumption? She was young, recently married,

fresh and unhackneyed in society, and my imagination decked her out with everything that
was pure, lovely, innocent, and angelic in wom-
anhood. She was pointed out to me in the
theatre shortly after my arrival in Madrid. I
turned with eagerness to the original of the
picture that had ever remained hung up in sanctity in my mind. I found her still handsome,
though somewhat matronly in appearance, seated,
with her daughters, in the box of a fashionable
nobleman, younger than herself, rich in purse
but poor in intellect, and who was openly and no-
toriously her *cavalier servante*. The charm was
broken, the picture fell from the wall. She may
have the customs of a depraved country and licen-
tious state of society to excuse her; but I can
never think of her again in the halo of feminine
purity and loveliness that surrounded the Virgin
of Murillo."

During Irving's ministry he was twice
absent, briefly in Paris and London, and was
called to the latter place for consultation in
regard to the Oregon boundary dispute, in
the settlement of which he rendered valuable service. Space is not given me for
further quotations from Irving's brilliant
descriptions of court, characters, and society
in that revolutionary time, nor of his half-

melancholy pilgrimage to the southern scenes
of his former reveries.   But I will take a
page from a letter to his sister, Mrs. Paris,
describing his voyage from Barcelona to
Marseilles, which exhibits the lively susceptibility of the author and diplomat who
was then in his sixty-first year : —

" While I am writing at a table in the cabin, I
am sensible of the power of a pair of splendid
Spanish eyes which are occasionally flashing upon
me, and which almost seem to throw a light upon
the paper.   Since I cannot break the spell, I will
describe the owner of them.   She is a young
married lady, about four or five and twenty, middle sized, finely modeled, a Grecian outline of
face, a complexion sallow yet healthful, raven
black hair, eyes dark, large, and beaming, softened by long eyelashes, lips full and rosy red,
yet finely chiseled, and teeth of dazzling whiteness.   She is dressed in black, as if in mourning;
on one hand is a black glove; the other hand,
ungloved, is small, exquisitely formed, with taper
fingers and blue veins.   She has just put it up
to adjust her clustering black locks.   I never saw
female hand more exquisite.   Really, if I were a
young man, I should not be able to draw the portrait of this beautiful creature so calmly.

" I was interrupted in my letter writing, by an

observation of the lady whom I was describing.
She had caught my eye occasionally, as it glanced
from my letter toward her. 'Really, Señor,'
said she, at length, with a smile, 'one would think
you were a painter taking my likeness.' I could
not resist the impulse. 'Indeed,' said I, 'I am
taking it; I am writing to a friend the other side
of the world, discussing things that are passing
before me, and I could not help noting down one
of the best specimens of the country that I had
met with.' A little bantering took place between
the young lady, her husband, and myself, which
ended in my reading off, as well as I could into
Spanish, the description I had just written down.
It occasioned a world of merriment, and was taken
in excellent part. The lady's cheek, for once,
mantled with the rose. She laughed, shook her
head, and said I was a very fanciful portrait
painter; and the husband declared that, if I would
stop at St. Filian, all the ladies in the place would
crowd to have their portraits taken, — my pictures
were so flattering. I have just parted with them.
The steamship stopped in the open sea, just in
front of the little bay of St. Filian; boats came
off from shore for the party. I helped the beautiful original of the portrait into the boat, and
promised her and her husband if ever I should
come to St. Filian I would pay them a visit. The
last I noticed of her was a Spanish farewell wave

of her beautiful white hand, and the gleam of her dazzling teeth as she smiled adieu. So there's a very tolerable touch of romance for a gentleman of my years."

When Irving announced his recall from the court of Madrid, the young Queen said to him in reply: "You may take with you into private life the intimate conviction that your frank and loyal conduct has contributed to draw closer the amicable relations which exist between North America and the Spanish nation, and that your distinguished personal merits have gained in my heart the appreciation which you merit by more than one title." The author was anxious to return. From the midst of court life in April, 1845, he had written: "I long to be once more back at dear little Sunnyside, while I have yet strength and good spirits to enjoy the simple pleasures of the country, and to rally a happy family group once more about me. I grudge every year of absence that rolls by. To-morrow is my birthday. I shall then be sixty-two years old. The evening of life is fast drawing over me; still I hope to get back among my friends while there is a little sunshine left."

It was the 19th of September, 1846, says his biographer, " when the impatient longing of his heart was gratified, and he found himself restored to his home for the thirteen years of happy life still remaining to him."

CHAPTER IX.

THE CHARACTERISTIC WORKS.

THE Knickerbocker's "History of New York" and the "Sketch-Book" never would have won for Irving the gold medal of the Royal Society of Literature, or the degree of D. C. L. from Oxford.

However much the world would have liked frankly to honor the writer for that which it most enjoyed and was under most obligations for, it would have been a violent shock to the constitution of things to have given such honor to the mere humorist and the writer of short sketches. The conventional literary proprieties must bo observed. Only some laborious, solid, and improving work of the pen could sanction such distinction, — a book of research or an historical composition. It need not necessarily be dull, but it must be grave in tone and serious in intention, in order to give the author high recognition.

Irving himself shared this opinion. He hoped, in the composition of his "Columbus" and his "Washington," to produce works which should justify the good opinion his countrymen had formed of him, should reasonably satisfy the expectations excited by his lighter books, and lay for him the basis of enduring reputation. All that he had done before was the play of careless genius, the exercise of frolicsome fancy, which might amuse and perhaps win an affectionate regard for the author, but could not justify a high respect or secure a permanent place in literature. For this, some work of scholarship and industry was needed.

And yet everybody would probably have admitted that there was but one man then living who could have created and peopled the vast and humorous world of the Knickerbockers; that all the learning of Oxford and Cambridge together would not enable a man to draw the whimsical portrait of Ichabod Crane, or to outline the fascinating legend of Rip Van Winkle; while Europe was full of scholars of more learning than Irving, and writers of equal skill in narrative, who

might have told the story of Columbus as
well as he told it and perhaps better. The
under-graduates of Oxford who hooted their
admiration of the shy author when he appeared in the theatre to receive his complimentary degree perhaps understood this,
and expressed it in their shouts of "Diedrich Knickerbocker," " Ichabod Crane,"
"Rip Van Winkle."

Irving's "gift" was humor; and allied to
this was sentiment. These qualities modified and restrained each other; and it was
by these that he touched the heart. He
acquired other powers which he himself
may have valued more highly, and which
brought him more substantial honors; but
the historical compositions, which he and
his contemporaries regarded as a solid basis
of fame, could be spared without serious
loss, while the works of humor, the first
fruits of his genius, are possessions in English literature the loss of which would be
irreparable. The world may never openly
allow to humor a position " above the salt,"
but it clings to its fresh and original productions, generation after generation, finding
room for them in its accumulating literary

baggage, while more "important" tomes of scholarship and industry strew the line of its march.

I feel that this study of Irving as a man of letters would be incomplete, especially for the young readers of this generation, if it did not contain some more extended citations from those works upon which we have formed our estimate of his quality. Wo will take first a few passages from the "History of New York."

It has been said that Irving lacked imagination. That, while he had humor and feeling and fancy, ho was wanting in the higher quality, which is the last test of genius. We have come to attach to the word "imagination" a larger meaning than the mere reproduction in the mind of certain absent objects of sense that have been perceived; there must be a suggestion of something beyond these, and an ennobling suggestion, if not a combination, that amounts to a new creation. Now, it seems to me that the transmutation of the crude and theretofore unpoetical materials, which he found in the New World, into what is as

13

absolute a creation as exists in literature, was a distinct work of the imagination. Its humorous quality does not interfere with its largeness of outline, nor with its essential poetic coloring. For, whimsical and comical as is the "Knickerbocker" creation, it is enlarged to the proportion of a realm, and over that new country of the imagination is always the rosy light of sentiment.

This largeness of modified conception cannot be made apparent in such brief extracts as we can make, but they will show its quality and the author's humor. The Low-Dutch settlers of the Nieuw Nederlandts are supposed to have sailed from Amsterdam in a ship called the Goede Vrouw, built by the carpenters of that city, who always model their ships on the fair forms of their countrywomen. This vessel, whose beauteous model was declared to be the greatest belle in Amsterdam, had one hundred feet in the beam, one hundred feet in the keel, and one hundred feet from the bottom of the stern-post to the taffrail. Those illustrious adventurers who sailed in her landed on the Jersey flats, preferring a marshy ground, where they could drive

piles and construct dykes. They made a
settlement at the Indian village of Communipaw, the egg from which was hatched the
mighty city of New York. In the author's
time this place had lost its importance: —

"Communipaw is at present but a small village, pleasantly situated, among rural scenery,
on that beauteous part of the Jersey shore which
was known in ancient legends by the name of
Pavonia,[1] and commands a grand prospect of the
superb bay of New York. It is within but half
an hour's sail of the latter place, provided you
have a fair wind, and may be distinctly seen from
the city. Nay, it is a well-known fact, which I
can testify from my own experience, that on a
clear still summer evening, you may hear, from
the Battery of New York, the obstreperous peals
of broad-mouthed laughter of the Dutch negroes
at Communipaw, who, like most other negroes,
are famous for their risible powers. This is pe-
culiarly the case on Sunday evenings, when, it is
remarked by an ingenious and observant philosopher, who has made great discoveries in the
neighborhood of this city, that they always laugh
loudest, which he attributes to the circumstance
of their having their holiday clothes on.

[1] Pavonia in the ancient maps, is given to a tract of
country extending from about Hoboken to Amboy.

" These negroes, in fact, like the monks of the dark ages, engross all the knowledge of the place, and being infinitely more adventurous and more knowing than their masters, carry on all the foreign trade; making frequent voyages to town in canoes loaded with oysters, buttermilk, and cabbages. They are great astrologers, predicting the different changes of weather almost as accurately as an almanac; they are moreover exquisite performers on three-stringed fiddles; in whistling they almost boast the far-famed powers of Orpheus's lyre, for not a horse or an ox in the place, when at the plough or before the wagon, will budge a foot until he hears the well-known whistle of his black driver and companion. And from their amazing skill at casting up accounts upon their fingers, they are regarded with as much veneration as were the disciples of Pythagoras of yore, when initiated into the sacred quaternary of numbers.

" As to the honest burghers of Communipaw, like wise men and sound philosophers, they never look beyond their pipes, nor trouble their heads about any affairs out of their immediate neighborhood; so that they live in profound and enviable ignorance of all the troubles, anxieties, and revolutions of this distracted planet. I am even told that many among them do verily believe that Holland, of which they have heard so much from

tradition, is situated somewhere on Long Island,
— that *Spiking-devil* and *the Narrows* are the
two ends of the world, — that the country is
still under the dominion of their High Mighti-
nesses, — and that the city of New York still goes
by the name of Nieuw Amsterdam. They meet
every Saturday afternoon at the only tavern in
the place, which bears as a sign a square-headed
likeness of the Prince of Orange, where they
smoke a silent pipe, by way of promoting social
conviviality, and invariably drink a mug of cider
to the success of Admiral Van Tromp, who they
imagine is still sweeping the British channel
with a broom at his mast-head.

" Communipaw, in short, is one of the numerous little villages in the vicinity of this most beautiful of cities, which are so many strongholds and
fastnesses, whither the primitive manners of our
Dutch forefathers have retreated, and where they
are cherished with devout and scrupulous strict-
ness. The dress of the original settlers is handed
down inviolate, from father to son : the identical
broad-brimmed hat, broad-skirted coat, and broad-
bottomed breeches, continue from generation to
generation ; and several gigantic knee-buckles of
massy silver are still in wear, that made gallant
display in the days of the patriarchs of Communipaw. The language likewise continues un-
adulterated by barbarous innovations ; and so

critically correct is the village schoolmaster in his
dialect, that his reading of a Low-Dutch psalm
has much the same effect on the nerves as the
filing of a handsaw."

The early prosperity of this settlement
is dwelt on with satisfaction by the author : —

" The neighboring Indians in a short time became accustomed to the uncouth sound of the
Dutch language, and an intercourse gradually
took place between them and the new-comers.
The Indians were much given to long talks, and
the Dutch to long silence ; — in this particular,
therefore, they accommodated each other completely.   The chiefs would make long speeches
about the big bull, the Wabash, and the Great
Spirit, to which the others would listen very attentively, smoke their pipes, and grunt *yah*, *myn-
her*, — whereat the poor savages were wondrously
delighted.   They instructed the new settlers in
the best art of curing and smoking tobacco, while
the latter, in return, made them drunk with true
Hollands — and then taught them the art of
making bargains.

" A brisk trade for furs was soon opened ; the
Dutch traders were scrupulously honest in their
dealings and purchased by weight, establishing it
as an invariable table of avoirdupois, that the

hand of a Dutchman weighed one pound, and his foot two pounds. It is true, the simple Indians were often puzzled by the great disproportion between bulk and weight, for let them place a bundle of furs, never so large, in one scale, and a Dutchman put his hand or foot in the other, the bundle was sure to kick the beam; — never was a package of furs known to weigh more than two pounds in the market of Communipaw!

"This is a singular fact, — but I have it direct from my great-great-grandfather, who had risen to considerable importance in the colony, being promoted to the office of weigh-master, on account of the uncommon heaviness of his foot.

"The Dutch possessions in this part of the globe began now to assume a very thriving appearance, and were comprehended under the general title of Nieuw Nederlandts, on account, as the Sage Vander Donck observes, of their great resemblance to the Dutch Netherlands, — which indeed was truly remarkable, excepting that the former were rugged and mountainous, and the latter level and marshy. About this time the tranquillity of the Dutch colonists was doomed to suffer a temporary interruption. In 1614, Captain Sir Samuel Argal, sailing under a commission from Dale, governor of Virginia, visited the Dutch settlements on Hudson River, and demanded their submission to the English crown

and Virginian dominion. To this arrogant demand, as they were in no condition to resist it,
they submitted for the time, like discreet and
reasonable men.

"It does not appear that the valiant Argal
molested the settlement of Communipaw; on
the contrary, I am told that when his vessel first
hove in sight, the worthy burghers were seized
with such a panic, that they fell to smoking their
pipes with astonishing vehemence; insomuch that
they quickly raised a cloud, which, combining
with the surrounding woods and marshes, completely enveloped and concealed their beloved village, and overhung the fair regions of Pavonia
— so that the terrible Captain Argal passed on
totally unsuspicious that a sturdy little Dutch settlement lay snugly couched in the mud, under
cover of all this pestilent vapor. In commemo-
ration of this fortunate escape, the worthy inhabitants have continued to smoke, almost without
intermission, unto this very day; which is said
to be the cause of the remarkable fog which
often hangs over Communipaw of a clear afternoon."

The golden age of New York was under
the reign of Walter Van Twiller, the first
governor of the province, and the best it
ever had. In his sketch of this excellent

magistrate Irving has embodied the abundance and tranquillity of those halcyon days : —

" The renowned Wouter (or Walter) Van Twiller was descended from a long line of Dutch burgomasters, who had successively dozed away their lives, and grown fat upon the bench of magistracy in Rotterdam ; and who had comported themselves with such singular wisdom and propriety, that they were never either heard or talked of — which, next to being universally applauded, should be the object of ambition of all magistrates and rulers. There are two opposite ways by which some men make a figure in the world : one, by talking faster than they think, and the other, by holding their tongues and not thinking at all. By the first, many a smatterer acquires the reputation of a man of quick parts ; by the other, many a dunderpate, like the owl, the stupidest of birds, comes to be considered the very type of wisdom. This, by the way, is a casual remark, which I would not, for the universe, have it thought I apply to Governor Van Twiller. It is true he was a man shut up within himself, like an oyster, and rarely spoke, except in monosyllables ; but then it was allowed he seldom said a foolish thing. So invincible was his gravity that he was never known to laugh or

even to smile through the whole course of a long
and prosperous life. Nay, if a joke were uttered
in his presence, that set light-minded hearers in
a roar, it was observed to throw him into a state
of perplexity.   Sometimes he would deign to inquire into the matter, and when, after much ex-
planation, the joke was made as plain as a pike-
staff, he would continue to smoke his pipe in
silence, and at length, knocking out the ashes,
would exclaim, ' Well ! I see nothing in all that
to laugh about.'

"With all his reflective habits, he never made
up his mind on a subject.   His adherents accounted for this by the astonishing magnitude of
his ideas.   He conceived every subject on so
grand a scale that he had not room in his head
to turn it over and examine both sides of it.
Certain it is, that, if any matter were propounded
to him on which ordinary mortals would rashly
determine at first glance, he would put on a
vague, mysterious look, shake his capacious
head, smoke some time in profound silence, and
at length observe, that ' he had his doubts about
the matter '; which gained him the reputation
of a man slow of belief and not easily imposed
upon.   What is more, it has gained him a lasting
name ; for to this habit of the mind has been
attributed his surname of Twiller ; which is said
to be a corruption of the original Twijfler, or,
in plain English, *Doubter*.

" The person of this illustrious old gentleman was formed and proportioned, as though it had been moulded by the hands of some cunning Dutch statuary, as a model of majesty and lordly grandeur. He was exactly five feet six inches in height, and six feet five inches in circumference. His head was a perfect sphere, and of such stupendous dimensions, that dame Nature, with all her sex's ingenuity, would have been puzzled to construct a neck capable of supporting it; wherefore she wisely declined the attempt, and settled it firmly on the top of his backbone, just between the shoulders. His body was oblong and particularly capacious at bottom; which was wisely ordered by Providence, seeing that he was a man of sedentary habits, and very averse to the idle labor of walking. His legs were short, but sturdy in proportion to the weight they had to sustain; so that when erect he had not a little the appearance of a beer-barrel on skids. His face, that infallible index of the mind, presented a vast expanse, unfurrowed by any of those lines and angles which disfigure the human countenance with what is termed expression. Two small gray eyes twinkled feebly in the midst, like two stars of lesser magnitude in a hazy firmament, and his full-fed cheeks, which seemed to have taken toll of everything that went into his mouth, were curiously mottled and streaked with dusky red, like a spitzenberg apple.

"His habits were as regular as his person.
He daily took his four stated meals, appropri-
ating exactly an hour to each; he smoked and
doubted eight hours, and he slept the remaining
twelve of the four-and-twenty. Such was the
renowned Wouter Van Twiller, — a true philosopher, for his mind was either elevated above, or
tranquilly settled below, the cares and perplexities
of this world. He had lived in it for years, without feeling the least curiosity to know whether
the sun revolved round it, or it round the sun;
and he had watched, for at least half a century,
the smoke curling from his pipe to the ceiling,
without once troubling his head with any of
those numerous theories by which a philosopher
would have perplexed his brain, in accounting
for its rising above the surrounding atmosphere.

"In his council he presided with great state
and solemnity. He sat in a huge chair of solid
oak, hewn in the celebrated forest of the Hague,
fabricated by an experienced timmerman of
Amsterdam, and curiously carved about the
arms and feet into exact imitations of gigantic
eagle's claws. Instead of a sceptre, he swayed
a long Turkish pipe, wrought with jasmin and
amber, which had been presented to a stadtholder
of Holland at the conclusion of a treaty with one
of the petty Barbary powers. In this stately
chair would he sit, and this magnificent pipe

would he smoke, shaking his right knee with a constant motion, and fixing his eye for hours together upon a little print of Amsterdam, which hung in a black frame against the opposite wall of the council-chamber.   Nay, it has even been said, that when any deliberation of extraordinary length and intricacy was on the carpet, the renowned Wouter would shut his eyes for full two hours at a time, that he might not be disturbed by external objects; and at such times the internal commotion of his mind was evinced by certain regular guttural sounds, which his admirers declared were merely the noise of conflict, made by his contending doubts and opinions. . . .

"I have been the more anxious to delineate fully the person and habits of Wouter Van Twiller, from the consideration that he was not only the first but also the best governor that ever presided over this ancient and respectable province; and so tranquil and benevolent was his reign, that I do not find throughout the whole of it a single instance of any offender being brought to punishment, — a most indubitable sign of a merciful governor, and a case unparalleled, excepting in the reign of the illustrious King Log, from whom, it is hinted, the renowned Van Twiller was a lineal descendant.

"The very outset of the career of this excellent magistrate was distinguished by an example

of legal acumen that gave flattering presage of
a wise and equitable administration. The morning after he had been installed in office, and at
the moment that he was making his breakfast
from a prodigious earthen dish, filled with milk
and Indian pudding, he was interrupted by the
appearance of Wandle Schoonhoven, a very important old burgher of New Amsterdam, who com-
plained bitterly of one Barent Bleecker, inasmuch as he refused to come to a settlement of
accounts, seeing that there was a heavy balance
in favor of the said Wandle. Governor Van
Twiller, as I have already observed, was a man
of few words ; he was likewise a mortal enemy
to multiplying writings — or being disturbed at
his breakfast. Having listened attentively to
the statement of Wandle Schoonhoven, giving
an occasional grunt, as he shoveled a spoonful
of Indian pudding into his mouth, — either as a
sign that he relished the dish, or comprehended
the story, — he called unto him his constable,
and pulling out of his breeches-pocket a huge
jack-knife, dispatched it after the defendant as a
summons, accompanied by his tobacco-box as a
warrant.

"This summary process was as effectual in
those simple days as was the seal-ring of the
great Haroun Alraschid among the true believers.
The two parties being confronted before him,

each produced a book of accounts, written in a
language and character that would have puzzled
any but a High-Dutch commentator, or a learned
decipherer of Egyptian obelisks. The sage Wouter took them one after the other, and having
poised them in his hands, and attentively counted
over the number of leaves, fell straightway into
a very great doubt, and smoked for half an hour
without saying a word; at length, laying his
finger beside his nose, and shutting his eyes for
a moment, with the air of a man who has just
caught a subtle idea by the tail, he slowly took
his pipe from his mouth, puffed forth a column
of tobacco-smoke, and with marvelous gravity
and solemnity pronounced, that, having carefully
counted over the leaves and weighed the books,
it was found, that one was just as thick and as
heavy as the other : therefore, it was the final
opinion of the court that the accounts were
equally balanced : therefore, Wandle should give
Barent a receipt, and Barent should give Wandle a receipt, and the constable should pay the
costs.

"This decision, being straightway made
known, diffused general joy throughout New
Amsterdam, for the people immediately perceived that they had a very wise and equitable
magistrate to rule over them. But its happiest
effect was, that not another lawsuit took place

throughout the whole of his administration; and
the office of constable fell into such decay, that
there was not one of those losel scouts known in
the province for many years. I am the more
particular in dwelling on this transaction, not
only because I deem it one of the most sage and
righteous judgments on record, and well worthy
the attention of modern magistrates, but because
it was a miraculous event in the history of the
renowned Wouter — being the only time he was
ever known to come to a decision in the whole
course of his life."

This peaceful age ended with the accession of William the Testy, and the advent
of the enterprising Yankees. During the
reigns of William Kieft and Peter Stuyvesant, between the Yankees of the Connecti-
cut and the Swedes of the Delaware, the
Dutch community knew no repose, and the
"History" is little more than a series of
exhausting sieges and desperate battles,
which would have been as heroic as any in
history if they had been attended with loss
of life. The forces that were gathered by
Peter Stuyvesant for the expedition to
avenge upon the Swedes the defeat at Fort
Casimir, and their appearance on the march,

give some notion of the military prowess of the Dutch. Their appearance, when they were encamped on the Bowling Green, recalls the Homeric age : —

" In the centre, then, was pitched the tent of the men of battle of the Manhattoes, who, being the inmates of the metropolis, composed the life-guards of the governor. These were commanded by the valiant Stoffel Brinkerhoof, who, whilom had acquired such immortal fame at Oyster Bay ; they displayed as a standard a beaver *rampant* on a field of orange, being the arms of the province, and denoting the persevering industry and the amphibious origin of the Nederlands.

" On their right hand might be seen the vassals of that renowned Mynheer, Michael Paw, who lorded it over the fair regions of ancient Pavonia, and the lands away south even unto the Nave-sink mountains, and was moreover patroon of Gibbet Island. His standard was borne by his trusty squire, Cornelius Van Vorst ; consisting of a huge oyster *recumbent* upon a sea-green field ; being the armorial bearings of his favorite metropolis, Communipaw. He brought to the camp a stout force of warriors, heavily armed, being each clad in ten pair of linsey-woolsey breeches, and overshadowed by broad-brimmed beavers, with short pipes twisted in their hat-bands.

14

These were the men who vegetated in the mud along the shores of Pavonia, being of the race of genuine copperheads, and were fabled to have sprung from oysters.

"At a little distance was encamped the tribe of warriors who came from the neighborhood of Hell-gate. These were commanded by the Suy Dams, and the Van Dams, — incontinent hard swearers, as their names betoken. They were terrible-looking fellows, clad in broad-skirted gaberdines, of that curious colored cloth called thunder and lightning, — and bore as a standard three devil's darning-needles, *volant*, in a flame-colored field.

"Hard by was the tent of the men of battle from the marshy borders of the Waale-Boght and the country thereabouts. These were of a sour aspect, by reason that they lived on crabs, which abound in these parts. They were the first institutors of that honorable order of knighthood called *Fly-market shirks*, and, if tradition speak true, did likewise introduce the far-famed step in dancing called 'double trouble.' They were commanded by the fearless Jacobus Varra Vanger, — and had, moreover, a jolly band of Breuckelen ferry-men, who performed a brave concerto on conch shells.

"But I refrain from pursuing this minute description, which goes on to describe the warriors of Bloemen-dael, and Weehawk, and Hoboken, and sundry other places, well known in history and song; for now do the notes of martial music alarm the people of New Amsterdam, sounding afar from beyond the walls of the city. But this alarm was in a little while relieved, for lo! from the midst of a vast cloud of dust, they recognized the brimstone-colored breeches and splendid silver leg of Peter Stuyvesant, glaring in the sunbeams; and beheld him approaching at the head of a formidable army, which he had mustered along the banks of the Hudson. And here the excellent but anonymous writer of the Stuyvesant manuscript breaks out into a brave and glorious description of the forces, as they defiled through the principal gate of the city, that stood by the head of Wall Street.

" First of all came the Van Bummels, who inhabit the pleasant borders of the Bronx: these were short fat men, wearing exceeding large trunk-breeches, and were renowned for feats of the trencher. They were the first inventors of suppawn, or mush and milk. — Close in their rear marched the Van Vlotens, of Kaatskill, horrible quaffers of new cider, and arrant braggarts in their liquor. — After them came the Van Pelts of Groodt Esopus, dexterous horsemen, mounted upon goodly switch-tailed steeds of the Esopus breed. These were mighty hunters of minks and

musk-rats, whence came the word *Peltry.* — Then
the Van Nests of Kinderhoeck, valiant robbers
of birds'-nests, as their name denotes. To these,
if report may be believed, are we indebted for
the invention of slap-jacks, or buckwheat-cakes.
— Then the Van Higginbottoms, of Wapping's
creek. These came armed with ferules and
birchen rods, being a race of schoolmasters, who
first discovered the marvelous sympathy between
the seat of honor and the seat of intellect, — and
that the shortest way to get knowledge into the
head was to hammer it into the bottom. — Then
the Van Grolls, of Antony's Nose, who carried
their liquor in fair round little pottles, by reason
they could not bouse it out of their canteens,
having such rare long noses. — Then the Gardeniers, of Hudson and thereabouts, distinguished
by many triumphant feats, such as robbing water-
melon patches, smoking rabbits out of their holes,
and the like, and by being great lovers of roasted
pigs' tails. These were the ancestors of the renowned congressman of that name. — Then the
Van Hoesens, of Sing-Sing, great choristers and
players upon the jews-harp. These marched two
and two, singing the great song of St. Nicholas.
— Then the Couenhovens, of Sleepy Hollow.
These gave birth to a jolly race of publicans,
who first discovered the magic artifice of conjur-
ing a quart of wine into a pint bottle. — Then

the Van Kortlandts, who lived on the wild banks of the Croton, and were great killers of wild ducks, being much spoken of for their skill in shooting with the long bow. — Then the Van Bunschotens, of Nyack and Kakiat, who were the first that did ever kick with the left foot. They were gallant bushwhackers and hunters of raccoons by moonlight. — Then the Van Winkles, of Haerlem, potent suckers of eggs, and noted for running of horses, and running up of scores at taverns. They were the first that ever winked with both eyes at once. — Lastly came the KNICKERBOCKERS, of the great town of Scagh-tikoke, where the folk lay stones upon the houses in windy weather, lest they should be blown away. These derive their name, as some say, from *Knicker*, to shake, and *Beker*, a goblet, indi-cating thereby that they were sturdy toss-pots of yore; but, in truth, it was derived from *Knicker*, to nod, and *Boeken*, books : plainly meaning that they were great nodders or dozers over books. From them did descend the writer of this his-tory."

In the midst of Irving's mock-heroics, he always preserves a substratum of good sense. An instance of this is the address of the redoubtable wooden-legged governor, on his departure at the head of his war-riors to chastise the Swedes : —

"Certain it is, not an old woman in New Amsterdam but considered Peter Stuyvesant as a tower of strength, and rested satisfied that the public welfare was secure so long as he was in the city. It is not surprising, then, that they looked upon his departure as a sore affliction. With heavy hearts they draggled at the heels of his troop, as they marched down to the river-side to embark. The governor, from the stern of his schooner, gave a short but truly patriarchal address to his citizens, wherein he recommended them to comport like loyal and peaceable subjects, — to go to church regularly on Sundays, and to mind their business all the week besides. That the women should be dutiful and affectionate to their husbands, — looking after nobody's concerns but their own, — eschewing all gossipings and morning gaddings, — and carrying short tongues and long petticoats. That the men should abstain from intermeddling in public concerns, intrusting the cares of government to the officers appointed to support them, — staying at home, like good citizens, making money for themselves, and getting children for the benefit of their country. That the burgomasters should look well to the public interest, — not oppressing the poor nor indulging the rich, — not tasking their ingenuity to devise new laws, but faithfully enforcing those which were already made, — rather bend-ing their attention to prevent evil than to punish it; ever recollecting that civil magistrates should consider themselves more as guardians of public morals than rat-catchers employed to entrap public delinquents. Finally, he exhorted them, one and all, high and low, rich and poor, to conduct themselves *as well as they could*, assuring them that if they faithfully and conscientiously complied with this golden rule, there was no danger but that they would all conduct themselves well enough. This done, he gave them a paternal benediction, the sturdy Antony sounded a most loving farewell with his trumpet, the jolly crews put up a shout of triumph, and the invincible armada swept off proudly down the bay."

The account of an expedition against Fort Christina deserves to be quoted in full, for it is an example of what war might be, full of excitement, and exercise, and heroism, without danger to life. We take up the narrative at the moment when the Dutch host, —

"Brimful of wrath and cabbage," —

and excited by the eloquence of the mighty Peter, lighted their pipes, and charged upon the fort.

"The Swedish garrison, ordered by the cunning Risingh not to fire until they could distinguish the whites of their assailants' eyes, stood in horrid silence on the covert-way, until the eager Dutchmen had ascended the glacis. Then did they pour into them such a tremendous volley, that the very hills quaked around, and were terrified even unto an incontinence of water, insomuch that certain springs burst forth from their sides, which continue to run unto the present day. Not a Dutchman but would have bitten the dust beneath that dreadful fire, had not the protecting Minerva kindly taken care that the Swedes should, one and all, observe their usual custom of shutting their eyes and turning away their heads at the moment of discharge.

" The Swedes followed up their fire by leaping the counterscarp, and falling tooth and nail upon the foe with curious outcries. And now might be seen prodigies of valor, unmatched in history or song. Here was the sturdy Stoffel Brinkerhoff brandishing his quarter-staff, like the giant Blanderon his oak-tree (for he scorned to carry any other weapon), and drumming a horrific tune upon the hard heads of the Swedish soldiery. There were the Van Kortlandts, posted at a distance, like the Locrian archers of yore, and plying it most potently with the long-bow, for which they were so justly renowned. On a rising knoll were gathered the valiant men of Sing-Sing, assisting marvelously in the fight by chanting the great song of St. Nicholas ; but as to the Gardeniers of Hudson, they were absent on a marauding party, laying waste the neighboring water-melon patches.

" In a different part of the field were the Van Grolls of Antony's Nose, struggling to get to the thickest of the fight, but horribly perplexed in a defile between two hills, by reason of the length of their noses. So also the Van Bunschotens of Nyack and Kakiat, so renowned for kicking with the left foot, were brought to a stand for want of wind, in consequence of the hearty dinner they had eaten, and would have been put to utter rout but for the arrival of a gallant corps of voltigeurs, composed of the Hoppers, who advanced nimbly to their assistance on one foot. Nor must I omit to mention the valiant achievements of Antony Van Corlear, who, for a good quarter of an hour, waged stubborn fight with a little pursy Swedish drummer, whose hide he drummed most magnificently, and whom he would infallibly have annihilated on the spot, but that he had come into the battle with no other weapon but his trumpet.

" But now the combat thickened. On came the mighty Jacobus Varra Vanger and the fighting-men of the Wallabout ; after them thundered the Van Pelts of Esopus, together with the Van Rippers and the Van Brunts, bearing down all before them; then the Suy Dams, and the Van Dams, pressing forward with many a blustering oath, at the head of the warriors of Hell-gate, clad in their thunder-and-lightning gaberdines; and lastly, the standard-bearers and body-guard of Peter Stuyvesant, bearing the great beaver of the Manhattoes.

"And now commenced the horrid din, the desperate struggle, the maddening ferocity, the frantic desperation, the confusion and self-abandonment of war. Dutchman and Swede commingled, tugged, panted, and blowed. The heavens were darkened with a tempest of missiles. Bang! went the guns; whack! went the broad-swords; thump! went the cudgels; crash! went the musket-stocks; blows, kicks, cuffs, scratches, black eyes and bloody noses swelling the horrors of the scene! Thick thwack, cut and hack, helter-skelter, higgledy-piggledy, hurly-burly, head-over-heels, rough-and-tumble! Dunder and blixum! swore the Dutchmen; splitter and splutter! cried the Swedes. Storm the works! shouted Hardkoppig Peter. Fire the mine! roared stout Risingh. Tanta-rar-ra-ra! twanged the trumpet of Antony Van Corlear; — until all voice and sound became unintelligible, — grunts of pain, yells of fury, and shouts of triumph mingling in one hideous clamor. The earth shook as if struck with a paralytic stroke; trees shrunk aghast, and withered at the sight; rocks burrowed in the ground like rabbits; and even Christina Creek turned from its course and ran up a hill in breathless terror!

"Long hung the contest doubtful; for though a heavy shower of rain, sent by the "cloud-compelling Jove," in some measure cooled their ardor, as doth a bucket of water thrown on a group of fighting mastiffs, yet did they but pause for a moment, to return with tenfold fury to the charge. Just at this juncture a vast and dense column of smoke was seen slowly rolling toward the scene of battle. The combatants paused for a moment, gazing in mute astonishment, until the wind, dispelling the murky cloud, revealed the flaunting banner of Michael Paw, the Patroon of Communipaw. That valiant chieftain came fearlessly on at the head of a phalanx of oyster-fed Pavonians and a *corps de reserve* of the Van Arsdales and Van Bummels, who had remained behind to digest the enormous dinner they had eaten. These now trudged manfully forward, smoking their pipes with outrageous vigor, so as to raise the awful cloud that has been mentioned, but marching exceedingly slow, being short of leg, and of great rotundity in the belt.

"And now the deities who watched over the

fortunes of the Nederlanders having unthinkingly left the field, and stepped into a neighboring tavern to refresh themselves with a pot of beer, a direful catastrophe had wellnigh ensued. Scarce had the myrmidons of Michael Paw attained the front of battle, when the Swedes, instructed by the cunning Risingh, leveled a shower of blows full at their tobacco-pipes. Astounded at this assault, and dismayed at the havoc of their pipes, these ponderous warriors gave way, and like a drove of frightened elephants broke through the ranks of their own army. The little Hoppers were borne down in the surge; the sacred banner emblazoned with the gigantic oyster of Communipaw was trampled in the dirt; on blundered and thundered the heavy-sterned fugitives, the Swedes pressing on their rear and applying their feet *a parte poste* of the Van Arsdales and the Van Bummels with a vigor that prodigiously accelerated their movements; nor did the renowned Michael Paw himself fail to receive divers grievous and dishonorable visitations of shoe-leather.

"But what, oh Muse! was the rage of Peter Stuyvesant, when from afar he saw his army giving way! In the transports of his wrath he sent forth a roar, enough to shake the very hills. The men of the Manhattoes plucked up new courage at the sound, or, rather, they rallied at

the voice of their leader, of whom they stood
more in awe than of all the Swedes in Christendom. Without waiting for their aid, the daring
Peter dashed, sword in hand, into the thickest of
the foe. Then might be seen achievements
worthy of the days of the giants. Wherever he
went the enemy shrank before him; the Swedes
fled to right and left, or were driven, like dogs,
into their own ditch; but as he pushed forward,
singly with headlong courage, the foe closed behind and hung upon his rear. One aimed a blow
full at his heart; but the protecting power which
watches over the great and good turned aside
the hostile blade and directed it to a side-pocket,
where reposed an enormous iron tobacco-box,
endowed, like the shield of Achilles, with supernatural powers, doubtless from bearing the portrait of the blessed St. Nicholas. Peter Stuyvesant turned like an angry bear upon the foe, and
seizing him, as he fled, by an immeasurable queue,
' Ah, whoreson caterpillar,' roared he, ' here 's
what shall make worms' meat of thee!' so saying he whirled his sword and dealt a blow that
would have decapitated the varlet, but that the
pitying steel struck short and shaved the queue
forever from his crown. At this moment an
arquebusier leveled his piece from a neighboring
mound, with deadly aim; but the watchful Minerva, who had just stopped to tie up her garter,

seeing the peril of her favorite hero, sent old Boreas with his bellows, who, as the match descended to the pan, gave a blast that blew the priming from the touch-hole.

"Thus waged the fight, when the stout Risingh, surveying the field from the top of a little ravelin, perceived his troops banged, beaten, and kicked by the invincible Peter. Drawing his falchion, and uttering a thousand anathemas, he strode down to the scene of combat with some such thundering strides as Jupiter is said by Hesiod to have taken when he strode down the spheres to hurl his thunder-bolts at the Titans.

"When the rival heroes came face to face, each made a prodigious start in the style of a veteran stage-champion. Then did they regard each other for a moment with the bitter aspect of two furious ram-cats on the point of a clapper-clawing. Then did they throw themselves into one attitude, then into another, striking their swords on the ground, first on the right side, then on the left: at last at it they went with incredible ferocity. Words cannot tell the prodigies of strength and valor displayed in this direful encounter, — an encounter compared to which the far-famed battles of Ajax with Hector, of Æneas with Turnus, Orlando with Rodomont, Guy of Warwick with Colbrand the Dane, or of that renowned Welsh knight, Sir Owen of the Mountains, with the giant Guylon, were all gentle sports and holiday recreations. At length the valiant Peter, watching his opportunity, aimed a blow enough to cleave his adversary to the very chine; but Risingh, nimbly raising his sword, warded it off so narrowly, that, glancing on one side, it shaved away a huge canteen in which he carried his liquor, — thence pursuing its trenchant course, it severed off a deep coat-pocket, stored with bread and cheese, — which provant, rolling among the armies, occasioned a fearful scrambling between the Swedes and Dutchmen, and made the general battle to wax more furious than ever.

" Enraged to see his military stores laid waste, the stout Risingh, collecting all his forces, aimed a mighty blow full at the hero's crest. In vain did his fierce little cocked hat oppose its course. The biting steel clove through the stubborn ram beaver, and would have cracked the crown of any one not endowed with supernatural hardness of head; but the brittle weapon shivered in pieces on the skull of Hardkoppig Piet, shedding a thousand sparks, like beams of glory, round his grizzly visage.

" The good Peter reeled with the blow, and turning up his eyes beheld a thousand suns, besides moons and stars, dancing about the firmament; at length, missing his footing, by reason of his wooden leg, down he came on his seat of honor with a crash which shook the surrounding hills, and might have wrecked his frame, had he not been received into a cushion softer than velvet, which Providence, or Minerva, or St. Nicholas, or some cow, had benevolently prepared for his reception.

"The furious Risingh, in despite of the maxim, cherished by all true knights, that 'fair play is a jewel,' hastened to take advantage of the hero's fall; but, as he stooped to give a fatal blow, Peter Stuyvesant dealt him a thwack over the sconce with his wooden leg, which set a chime of bells ringing triple bob-majors in his cerebellum. The bewildered Swede staggered with the blow, and the wary Peter seizing a pocket-pistol, which lay hard by, discharged it full at the head of the reeling Risingh. Let not my reader mistake; it was not a murderous weapon loaded with powder and ball, but a little sturdy stone pottle charged to the muzzle with a double dram of true Dutch courage, which the knowing Antony Van Corlear carried about him by way of replenishing his valor, and which had dropped from his wallet during his furious encounter with the drummer. The hideous weapon sang through the air, and true to its course as was the fragment of a rock discharged at Hector by bully Ajax, encountered the head of the gigantic Swede with matchless violence.

"This heaven-directed blow decided the battle. The ponderous pericranium of General Jan Rising sank upon his breast; his knees tottered under him; a deathlike torpor seized upon his frame, and he tumbled to the earth with such violence that old Pluto started with affright, lest he should have broken through the roof of his infernal palace.

"His fall was the signal of defeat and victory: the Swedes gave way, the Dutch pressed forward; the former took to their heels, the latter hotly pursued. Some entered with them, pell-mell, through the sally-port; others stormed the bastion, and others scrambled over the curtain. Thus in a little while the fortress of Fort Christina, which, like another Troy, had stood a siege of full ten hours, was carried by assault, without the loss of a single man on either side. Victory, in the likeness of a gigantic ox-fly, sat perched upon the cocked hat of the gallant Stuyvesant; and it was declared by all the writers whom he hired to write the history of his expedition that on this memorable day he gained a sufficient quantity of glory to immortalize a dozen of the greatest heroes in Christendom!"

In the "Sketch-Book," Irving set a kind of fashion in narrative essays, in brief stories of mingled humor and pathos, which

15

was followed for half a century. He him-self worked the same vein in " Bracebridge Hall," and " Tales of a Traveller." And there is no doubt that some of the most fascinating of the minor sketches of Charles Dickens, such as the story of the Bagman's Uncle, are lineal descendants of, if they were not suggested by, Irving's " Adven-ture of My Uncle," and the " Bold Dra-goon."

The taste for the leisurely description and reminiscent essay of the " Sketch-Book " does not characterize the readers of this generation, and we have discovered that the pathos of its elaborated scenes is somewhat " literary." The sketches of " Little Britain," and " Westminster Ab-bey," and, indeed, that of " Stratford-on-Avon," will for a long time retain their place in selections of " good reading; " but the " Sketch-Book " is only floated, as an original work, by two papers, the " Rip Van Winkle " and the " Legend of Sleepy Hol-low; " that is to say by the use of the Dutch material, and the elaboration of the " Knickerbocker Legend," which was the great achievement of Irving's life. This was broadened and deepened and illustrated by the several stories of the " Money Diggers," of " Wolfert Webber " and " Kidd the Pirate," in " The Tales of a Traveller," and by " Dolph Heyliger " in " Bracebridge Hall." Irving was never more successful than in painting the Dutch manners and habits of the early time, and he returned again and again to the task until he not only made the shores of the Hudson and the islands of New York harbor and the East River classic ground, but until his conception of Dutch life in the New World had assumed historical solidity and become a tradition of the highest poetic value. If in the multiplicity of books and the change of taste the bulk of Irving's works shall go out of print, a volume made up of his Knickerbocker history and the legends relating to the region of New York and the Hudson would survive as long as anything that has been produced in this country.

The philosophical student of the origin of New World society may find food for reflection in the " materiality " of the basis of the civilization of New York. The picture of abundance and of enjoyment of animal life is perhaps not overdrawn in Irving's sketch of the home of the Van Tassels, in " The Legend of Sleepy Hollow." It is all the extract we can make room for from that careful study : —

" Among the musical disciples who assembled, one evening in each week, to receive his instructions in psalmody, was Katrina Van Tassel, the daughter and only child of a substantial Dutch farmer. She was a blooming lass of fresh eighteen ; plump as a partridge ; ripe and melting and rosy-cheeked as one of her father's peaches, and universally famed, not merely for her beauty, but her vast expectations. She was, withal, a little of a coquette, as might be perceived even in her dress, which was a mixture of ancient and modern fashions, as most suited to set off her charms. She wore the ornaments of pure yellow gold which her great-great-grandmother had brought over from Saardam ; the tempting stomacher of the olden time ; and withal a provokingly short petticoat, to display the prettiest foot and ankle in the country round.

" Ichabod Crane had a soft and foolish heart towards the sex ; and it is not to be wondered at that so tempting a morsel soon found favor in his eyes, more especially after he had visited her in her paternal mansion. Old Baltus Van Tassel was a perfect picture of a thriving, contented, liberal-hearted farmer. He seldom, it is true, sent either his eyes or his thoughts beyond the boundaries of his own farm; but within those everything was snug, happy, and well-conditioned. He was satisfied with his wealth, but not proud of it; and piqued himself upon the hearty abundance rather than the style in which he lived. His stronghold was situated on the banks of the Hudson, in one of those green, sheltered, fertile nooks in which the Dutch farmers are so fond of nestling. A great elm-tree spread its broad branches over it, at the foot of which bubbled up a spring of the softest and sweetest water, in a little well, formed of a barrel, and then stole sparkling away through the grass to a neighboring brook, that bubbled along among alders and dwarf willows. Hard by the farm-house was a vast barn, that might have served for a church, every window and crevice of which seemed bursting forth with the treasures of the farm. The flail was busily resounding within it from morning till night; swallows and martins skimmed twittering about the eaves; and rows of pigeons, some with one eye turned up, as if watching the weather, some with their heads under their wings, or buried in their bosoms, and others swelling and cooing and bowing about their dames, were enjoying the sunshine on the roof. Sleek, unwieldy porkers were grunting in the repose and abundance of their pens, whence sallied forth, now and then, troops of sucking pigs, as if to snuff the air. A stately squadron of snowy geese were riding in an adjoining pond, convoying whole fleets of ducks; regiments of turkeys were gobbling through the farm-yard, and guinea fowls fretting about it, like ill-tempered housewives, with their peevish, discontented cry. Before the barn door strutted the gallant cock, that pattern of a husband, a warrior, and a fine gentleman, clapping his burnished wings, and crowing in the pride and gladness of his heart — sometimes tearing up the earth with his feet, and then generously calling his ever-hungry family of wives and children to enjoy the rich morsel which he had discovered.

"The pedagogue's mouth watered as he looked upon this sumptuous promise of luxurious winter fare. In his devouring mind's eye he pictured to himself every roasting-pig running about with a pudding in his belly, and an apple in his mouth; the pigeons were snugly put to bed in a comfortable pie, and tucked in with a coverlet of crust; the geese were swimming in their own gravy, and the ducks pairing cosily in dishes, like snug married couples, with a decent competency of onion-sauce. In the porkers he saw carved out the future sleek side of bacon, and juicy relishing ham ; not a turkey but he beheld daintily trussed up, with its gizzard under its wing, and, peradventure, a necklace of savory sausages ; and even bright chanticleer himself lay sprawling on his back, in a side-dish, with uplifted claws, as if craving that quarter which his chivalrous spirit disdained to ask while living.

" As the enraptured Ichabod fancied all this, and as he rolled his great green eyes over the fat meadow-lands, the rich fields of wheat, of rye, of buckwheat, and Indian corn, and the orchard burdened with ruddy fruit, which surrounded the warm tenement of Van Tassel, his heart yearned after the damsel who was to inherit these domains, and his imagination expanded with the idea how they might be readily turned into cash, and the money invested in immense tracts of wild land and shingle palaces in the wilderness. Nay, his busy fancy already realized his hopes, and presented to him the blooming Katrina, with a whole family of children, mounted on the top of a wagon loaded with household trumpery, with pots and kettles dangling beneath ; and he beheld himself bestriding a pacing mare, with a colt at her heels, setting out for Kentucky, Tennessee, or the Lord knows where.

" When he entered the house, the conquest of his heart was complete. It was one of those spacious farm-houses, with high-ridged, but lowly·

sloping roofs, built in the style handed down from
the first Dutch settlers; the low projecting eaves
forming a piazza along the front, capable of being closed up in bad weather. Under this were
hung flails, harness, various utensils of husbandry,
and nets for fishing in the neighboring river.
Benches were built along the sides for summer
use; and a great spinning-wheel at one end, and
a churn at the other, showed the various uses to
which this important porch might be devoted.
From this piazza the wondering Ichabod entered
the hall, which formed the centre of the mansion
and the place of usual residence. Here, rows of
resplendent pewter, ranged on a long dresser,
dazzled his eyes. In one corner stood a huge
bag of wool ready to be spun; in another a quantity of linsey-woolsey just from the loom; ears
of Indian corn, and strings of dried apples and
peaches, hung in gay festoons along the walls,
mingled with the gaud of red peppers; and a
door left ajar gave him a peep into the best par-
lor, where the claw-footed chairs and dark ma-
hogany tables shone like mirrors; and irons, with
their accompanying shovel and tongs, glistened
from their covert of asparagus tops; mock-or-
anges and conch-shells decorated the mantel-
piece; strings of various colored birds' eggs were
suspended above it; a great ostrich egg was hung
from the centre of the room, and a corner cup-

board, knowingly left open, displayed immense treasures of old silver and well-mended china."

It is an abrupt transition from these homely scenes, which humor commends to our liking, to the chivalrous pageant unrolled for us in the " Conquest of Granada." The former are more characteristic and the more enduring of Irving's writings, but as a literary artist his genius lent itself just as readily to Oriental and mediæval romance as to the Knickerbocker legend; and there is no doubt that the delicate perception he had of chivalric achievements gave a refined tone to his mock heroics, which greatly heightened their effect. It may almost be claimed that Irving did for Granada and the Alhambra what he did, in a totally different way, for New York and its vicinity.

The first passage I take from the " Conquest " is the description of the advent at Cordova of the Lord Scales, Earl of Rivers, who was brother of the queen of Henry VII., a soldier who had fought at Bosworth field, and now volunteered to aid Ferdinand and Isabella in the extermination of the Saracens. The description is put into the mouth of Fray Antonio Agapida, a fictitious

chronicler invented by Irving, an unfortunate intervention which gives to the whole
book an air of unveracity : —

" ' This cavalier [he observes] was from the far
island of England, and brought with him a train
of his vassals ; men who had been hardened in
certain civil wars which raged in their country.
They were a comely race of men, but too fair
and fresh for warriors, not having the sunburnt,
warlike hue of our old Castilian soldiery. They
were huge feeders also, and deep carousers, and
could not accommodate themselves to the sober
diet of our troops, but must fain eat and drink
after the manner of their own country. They
were often noisy and unruly, also, in their was-
sail ; and their quarter of the camp was prone
to be a scene of loud revel and sudden brawl.
They were, withal, of great pride, yet it was not
like our inflammable Spanish pride : they stood
not much upon the *pundonor*, the high punctilio,
and rarely drew the stiletto in their disputes ; but
their pride was silent and contumelious. Though
from a remote and somewhat barbarous island,
they believed themselves the most perfect men
upon earth, and magnified their chieftain, the
Lord Scales, beyond the greatest of their grandees.
With all this, it must be said of them that they
were marvelous good men in the field, dexterous

archers, and powerful with the battle-axe. In
their great pride and self-will, they always sought
to press in the advance and take the post of danger, trying to outvie our Spanish chivalry. They
did not rush on fiercely to the fight, nor make
a brilliant onset like the Moorish and Spanish
troops, but they went into the fight deliberately,
and persisted obstinately, and were slow to find
out when they were beaten. Withal they were
much esteemed yet little liked by our soldiery,
who considered them staunch companions in the
field, yet coveted but little fellowship with them
in the camp.

"'Their commander, the Lord Scales, was an
accomplished cavalier, of gracious and noble
presence and fair speech ; it was a marvel to see
so much courtesy in a knight brought up so far
from our Castilian court. He was much honored
by the king and queen, and found great favor
with the fair dames about the court, who indeed
are rather prone to be pleased with foreign cavaliers. He went always in costly state, attended
by pages and esquires, and accompanied by noble
young cavaliers of his country, who had enrolled
themselves under his banner, to learn the gentle
exercise of arms. In all pageants and festivals,
the eyes of the populace were attracted by the
singular bearing and rich array of the English
earl and his train, who prided themselves in al-

ways appearing in the garb and manner of their country — and were indeed something very magnificent, delectable, and strange to behold.'

" The worthy chronicler is no less elaborate in his description of the masters of Santiago, Calatrava, and Alcantara, and their valiant knights, armed at all points, and decorated with the badges of their orders.   These, he affirms, were the flower of Christian chivalry ; being constantly in service they became more steadfast and accomplished in discipline than the irregular and temporary levies of feudal nobles.   Calm, solemn, and stately, they sat like towers upon their powerful chargers.   On parades they manifested none of the show and ostentation of the other troops : neither, in battle, did they endeavor to signalize themselves by any fiery vivacity, or desperate and vainglorious exploit, — everything, with them, was measured and sedate ; yet it was observed that none were more warlike in their appearance in the camp, or more terrible for their achievements in the field.

" The gorgeous magnificence of the Spanish nobles found but little favor in the eyes of the sovereigns.   They saw that it caused a competition in expense ruinous to cavaliers of moderate fortune ; and they feared that a softness and effeminacy might thus be introduced, incompatible with the stern nature of the war.   They signified their disapprobation to several of the principal noblemen, and recommended a more sober and soldier-like display while in actual service.

"'These are rare troops for a tournay, my lord [said Ferdinand to the Duke of Infantado, as he beheld his retainers glittering in gold and embroidery]; but gold, though gorgeous, is soft and yielding: iron is the metal for the field.'

"'Sire [replied the duke], if my men parade in gold, your majesty will find they fight with steel.' The king smiled, but shook his head, and the duke treasured up his speech in his heart."

Our author excels in such descriptions as that of the progress of Isabella to the camp of Ferdinand after the capture of Loxa, and of the picturesque pageantry which imparted something of gayety to the brutal pastime of war : —

"It was in the early part of June that the queen departed from Cordova, with the Princess Isabella and numerous ladies of her court. She had a glorious attendance of cavaliers and pages, with many guards and domestics. There were forty mules for the use of the queen, the princess, and their train.

"As this courtly cavalcade approached the Rock of the Lovers, on the banks of the river Yeguas, they beheld a splendid train of knights advancing to meet them. It was headed by that accomplished cavalier the Marques Duke de Cadiz, accompanied by the adelantado of Andalusia. He had left the camp the day after the capture of Illora, and advanced thus far to receive the queen and escort her over the borders. The queen received the marques with distinguished honor, for he was esteemed the mirror of chivalry. His actions in this war had become the theme of every tongue, and many hesitated not to compare him in prowess with the immortal Cid.

"Thus gallantly attended, the queen entered the vanquished frontier of Granada, journeying securely along the pleasant banks of the Xenel, so lately subject to the scourings of the Moors. She stopped at Loxa, where she administered aid and consolation to the wounded, distributing money among them for their support, according to their rank.

"The king, after the capture of Illora, had removed his camp before the fortress of Moclin, with an intention of besieging it. Thither the queen proceeded, still escorted through the mountain roads by the Marques of Cadiz. As Isabella drew near to the camp, the Duke del Infantado issued forth a league and a half to receive her, magnificently arrayed, and followed by all his chivalry in glorious attire. With him came the

standard of Seville, borne by the men-at-arms of
that renowned city, and the Prior of St. Juan,
with his followers. They ranged themselves in
order of battle, on the left of the road by which
the queen was to pass.

"The worthy Agapida is loyally minute in
his description of the state and grandeur of the
Catholic sovereigns. The queen rode a chestnut
mule, seated in a magnificent saddle-chair, decorated with silver gilt. The housings of the mule
were of fine crimson cloth ; the borders embroidered with gold; the reins and head-piece were
of satin, curiously embossed with needlework of
silk, and wrought with golden letters. The queen
wore a brial or regal skirt of velvet, under which
were others of brocade ; a scarlet mantle, ornamented in the Moresco fashion ; and a black hat,
embroidered round the crown and brim.

"The infanta was likewise mounted on a chestnut mule, richly caparisoned. She wore a brial
or skirt of black brocade, and a black mantle ornamented like that of the queen.

"When the royal cavalcade passed by the
chivalry of the Duke del Infantado, which was
drawn out in battle array, the queen made a rev-
erence to the standard of Seville, and ordered it
to pass to the right hand. When she approached
the camp, the multitude ran forth to meet her,
with great demonstrations of joy; for she was

universally beloved by her subjects. All the battalions sallied forth in military array, bearing the various standards and banners of the camp, which were lowered in salutation as she passed.

"The king now came forth in royal state, mounted on a superb chestnut horse, and attended by many grandees of Castile. He wore a jubon or close vest of crimson cloth, with cuisses or short skirts of yellow satin, a loose cassock of brocade, a rich Moorish scimiter, and a hat with plumes. The grandees who attended him were arrayed with wonderful magnificence, each according to his taste and invention.

"These high and mighty princes [says Antonio Agapida] regarded each other with great deference, as allied sovereigns rather than with connubial familiarity, as mere husband and wife. When they approached each other, therefore, before embracing, they made three profound reverences, the queen taking off her hat, and remaining in a silk net or cawl, with her face uncovered. The king then approached and embraced her, and kissed her respectfully on the cheek. He also embraced his daughter the princess; and, making the sign of the cross, he blessed her, and kissed her on the lips.

"The good Agapida seems scarcely to have been more struck with the appearance of the sovereigns than with that of the English earl. He followed [says he] immediately after the king, with great pomp, and, in an extraordinary manner, taking precedence of all the rest. He was mounted '*a la guisa*,' or with long stirrups, on a superb chestnut horse, with trappings of azure silk which reached to the ground. The housings were of mulberry, powdered with stars of gold. He was armed in proof, and wore over his armor a short French mantle of black brocade ; he had a white French hat with plumes, and carried on his left arm a small round buckler, banded with gold. Five pages attended him, apparelled in silk and brocade, and mounted on horses sumptuously caparisoned; he had also a train of followers, bravely attired after the fashion of his country.

" He advanced in a chivalrous and courteous manner, making his reverences first to the queen and infanta, and afterwards to the king. Queen Isabella received him graciously, complimenting him on his courageous conduct at Loxa, and condoling with him on the loss of his teeth. The earl, however, made light of his disfiguring wound, saying that 'our blessed Lord, who had built all that house, had opened a window there, that he might see more readily what passed within;' whereupon the worthy Fray Antonio Agapida is more than ever astonished at the pregnant wit of this island cavalier. The earl continued some

16

little distance by the side of the royal family, complimenting them all with courteous speeches, his horse curveting and caracoling, but being managed with great grace and dexterity, — leaving the grandees and the people at large not more filled with admiration at the strangeness and magnificence of his state than at the excellence of his horsemanship.

" To testify her sense of the gallantry and services of this noble English knight, who had come from so far to assist in their wars, the queen sent him the next day presents of twelve horses, with stately tents, fine linen, two beds with coverings of gold brocade, and many other articles of great value."

The protracted siege of the city of Granada was the occasion of feats of arms and hostile courtesies which rival in brilliancy any in the romances of chivalry. Irving's pen is never more congenially employed than in describing these desperate but romantic encounters. One of the most picturesque of these was known as " the queen's skirmish." The royal encampment was situated so far from Granada that only the general aspect of the city could be seen as it rose from the vega, covering the sides of the hills with its palaces and towers.

Queen Isabella expressed a desire for a nearer view of the city, whose beauty was renowned throughout the world, and the courteous Marques of Cadiz proposed to give her this perilous gratification.

" On the morning of June the 18th, a magnificent and powerful train issued from the Christian camp. The advanced guard was composed of legions of cavalry, heavily armed, looking like moving masses of polished steel. Then came the king and queen, with the prince and princesses, and the ladies of the court, surrounded by the royal body-guard, sumptuously arrayed, composed of the sons of the most illustrious houses of Spain ; after these was the rear-guard, a powerful force of horse and foot ; for the flower of the army sallied forth that day. The Moors gazed with fearful admiration at this glorious pageant, wherein the pomp of the court was mingled with the terrors of the camp. It moved along in radiant line, across the vega, to the melodious thunders of martial music, while banner and plume, and silken scarf, and rich brocade, gave a gay and gorgeous relief to the grim visage of iron war that lurked beneath.

" The army moved towards the hamlet of Zubia, built on the skirts of the mountain to the left of Granada, and commanding a view of the

Alhambra, and the most beautiful quarter of the city. As they approached the hamlet, the Marques of Villena, the Count Ureña, and Don Alonzo de Aguilar filed off with their battalions, and were soon seen glittering along the side of the mountain above the village. In the mean time the Marques of Cadiz, the Count de Tendilla, the Count de Cabra, and Don Alonzo Fernandez, senior of Alcaudrete and Montemayor, drew up their forces in battle array on the plain below the hamlet, presenting a living barrier of loyal chivalry between the sovereigns and the city.

" Thus securely guarded, the royal party alighted, and, entering one of the houses of the hamlet, which had been prepared for their reception, enjoyed a full view of the city from its terraced roof. The ladies of the court gazed with delight at the red towers of the Alhambra, rising from amid shady groves, anticipating the time when the Catholic sovereigns should be enthroned within its walls, and its courts shine with the splendor of Spanish chivalry. ' The reverend prelates and holy friars, who always surrounded the queen, looked with serene satisfaction,' says Fray Antonio Agapida, 'at this modern Babylon, enjoying the triumph that awaited them, when those mosques and minarets should be converted into churches, and goodly priests and bishops should succeed to the infidel alfaquis.'

"When the Moors beheld the Christians thus drawn forth in full array in the plain, they supposed it was to offer battle, and hesitated not to accept it. In a little while the queen beheld a body of Moorish cavalry pouring into the vega, the riders managing their fleet and fiery steeds with admirable address. They were richly armed, and clothed in the most brilliant colors, and the caparisons of their steeds flamed with gold and embroidery. This was the favorite squadron of Muza, composed of the flower of the youthful cavaliers of Granada. Others succeeded, some heavily armed, others *à la gineta*, with lance and buckler; and lastly came the legions of foot-soldiers, with arquebus and cross-bow, and spear and scimiter.

"When the queen saw this army issuing from the city, she sent to the Marques of Cadiz, and forbade any attack upon the enemy, or the acceptance of any challenge to a skirmish; for she was loth that her curiosity should cost the life of a single human being.

"The marques promised to obey, though sorely against his will; and it grieved the spirit of the Spanish cavaliers to be obliged to remain with sheathed swords while bearded by the foe. The Moors could not comprehend the meaning of this inaction of the Christians, after having apparently invited a battle. They sallied several times from their ranks, and approached near enough to discharge their arrows; but the Christians were immovable. Many of the Moorish horsemen galloped close to the Christian ranks, brandishing their lances and scimiters, and defying various cavaliers to single combat; but Ferdinand had rigorously prohibited all duels of this kind, and they dared not transgress his orders under his very eye.

" Here, however, the worthy Fray Antonio Agapida, in his enthusiasm for the triumphs of the faith, records the following incident, which we fear is not sustained by any grave chronicler of the times; but rests merely on tradition, or the authority of certain poets and dramatic writers, who have perpetuated the tradition in their works. While this grim and reluctant tranquillity prevailed along the Christian line, says Agapida, there rose a mingled shout and sound of laughter near the gate of the city. A Moorish horseman, armed at all points, issued forth, followed by a rabble, who drew back as he approached the scene of danger. The Moor was more robust and brawny than was common with his countrymen. His visor was closed; he bore a huge buckler and a ponderous lance; his scimiter was of a Damascus blade, and his richly ornamented dagger was wrought by an artificer of Fez. He was known by his device to be Tarfe, the most insolent, yet valiant, of the Moslem warriors — the same who had hurled into the royal camp his lance, inscribed to the queen. As he rode slowly along in front of the army, his very steed, prancing with fiery eye and distended nostril, seemed to breathe defiance to the Christians.

" But what were the feelings of the Spanish cavaliers when they beheld, tied to the tail of his steed, and dragged in the dust, the very inscription, 'AVE MARIA,' which Hernan Perez del Pulgar had affixed to the door of the mosque! A burst of horror and indignation broke forth from the army. Hernan was not at hand, to maintain his previous achievement; but one of his young companions in arms, Garcilasso de la Vega by name, putting spurs to his horse, galloped to the hamlet of Zubia, threw himself on his knees before the king, and besought permission to accept the defiance of this insolent infidel and to revenge the insult offered to our Blessed Lady. The request was too pious to be refused. Garcilasso remounted his steed, closed his helmet, graced by four sable plumes, grasped his buckler of Flemish workmanship, and his lance of matchless temper, and defied the haughty Moor in the midst of his career. A combat took place in view of the two armies and of the Castilian court. The Moor was powerful in wielding his

weapons, and dexterous in managing his steed.
He was of larger frame than Garcilasso, and
more completely armed, and the Christians trem-
bled for their champion. The shock of their
encounter was dreadful; their lances were shivered, and sent up splinters in the air. Garcilasso
was thrown back in his saddle — his horse made
a wide career before he could recover, gather up
the reins, and return to the conflict. They now
encountered each other with swords. The Moor
circled round his opponent, as a hawk circles
when about to make a swoop; his steed obeyed
his rider with matchless quickness; at every attack of the infidel, it seemed as if the Christian
knight must sink beneath his flashing scimiter.
But if Garcilasso was inferior to him in power,
he was superior in agility; many of his blows
he parried; others he received upon his Flemish
shield, which was proof against the Damascus
blade. The blood streamed from numerous
wounds received by either warrior. The Moor,
seeing his antagonist exhausted, availed himself
of his superior force, and, grappling, endeavored
to wrest him from his saddle. They both fell to
earth; the Moor placed his knee upon the breast
of his victim, and, brandishing his dagger, aimed
a blow at his throat. A cry of despair was uttered by the Christian warriors, when suddenly
they beheld the Moor rolling lifeless in the dust.

Garcilasso had shortened his sword, and, as his adversary raised his arm to strike, had pierced him to the heart. 'It was a singular and miraculous victory,' says Fray Antonio Agapida; 'but the Christian knight was armed by the sacred nature of his cause, and the Holy Virgin gave him strength, like another David, to slay this gigantic champion of the Gentiles.'

"The laws of chivalry were observed throughout the combat — no one interfered on either side. Garcilasso now despoiled his adversary; then, rescuing the holy inscription of 'AVE MARIA' from its degrading situation, he elevated it on the point of his sword, and bore it off as a signal of triumph, amidst the rapturous shouts of the Christian army.

"The sun had now reached the meridian, and the hot blood of the Moors was inflamed by its rays, and by the sight of the defeat of their champion. Muza ordered two pieces of ordnance to open a fire upon the Christians. A confusion was produced in one part of their ranks: Muza called to the chiefs of the army, 'Let us waste no more time in empty challenges — let us charge upon the enemy: he who assaults has always an advantage in the combat.' So saying, he rushed forward, followed by a large body of horse and foot, and charged so furiously upon the advance guard of the Christians, that he drove it in upon the battalion of the Marques of Cadiz.

"The gallant marques now considered himself absolved from all further obedience to the queen's commands. He gave the signal to attack. 'Santiago!' was shouted along the line; and he pressed forward to the encounter, with his battalion of twelve hundred lances. The other cavaliers followed his example, and the battle instantly became general.

"When the king and queen beheld the armies thus rushing to the combat, they threw themselves on their knees, and implored the Holy Virgin to protect her faithful warriors. The prince and princess, the ladies of the court, and the prelates and friars who were present, did the same; and the effect of the prayers of these illustrious and saintly persons was immediately apparent. The fierceness with which the Moors had rushed to the attack was suddenly cooled; they were bold and adroit for a skirmish, but unequal to the veteran Spaniards in the open field. A panic seized upon the foot-soldiers — they turned and took to flight. Muza and his cavaliers in vain endeavored to rally them. Some took refuge in the mountains; but the greater part fled to the city, in such confusion that they overturned and trampled upon each other. The Christians pursued them to the very gates. Upwards of two thousand were either killed, wounded, or taken prisoners; and the two pieces of ordnance were brought off as trophies of the victory. Not a Christian lance but was bathed that day in the blood of an infidel.

"Such was the brief but bloody action which was known among the Christian warriors by the name of "The Queen's Skirmish;" for when the Marques of Cadiz waited upon her majesty to apologize for breaking her commands, he attributed the victory entirely to her presence. The queen, however, insisted that it was all owing to her troops being led on by so valiant a commander. Her majesty had not yet recovered from her agitation at beholding so terrible a scene of bloodshed, though certain veterans present pronounced it as gay and gentle a skirmish as they had ever witnessed."

The charm of "The Alhambra" is largely in the leisurely, loitering, dreamy spirit in which the temporary American resident of the ancient palace-fortress entered into its mouldering beauties and romantic associations, and in the artistic skill with which he wove the commonplace daily life of his attendants there into the more brilliant woof of its past. The book abounds in delightful legends, and yet these are all so touched with the author's airy humor that our credulity is never overtaxed; we imbibe all the romantic interest of the place without for a moment losing our hold upon reality. The enchantments of this Moorish paradise become part of our mental possessions, without the least shock to our common sense. After a few days of residence in the part of the Alhambra occupied by Dame Tia Antonia and her family, of which the handmaid Dolores was the most fascinating member, Irving succeeded in establishing himself in a remote and vacant part of the vast pile, in a suite of delicate and elegant chambers, with secluded gardens and fountains, that had once been occupied by the beautiful Elizabeth of Farnese, daughter of the Duke of Parma, and more than four centuries ago by a Moorish beauty named Lindaraxa, who flourished in the court of Muhamed the Left-Handed. These solitary and ruined chambers had their own terrors and enchantments, and for the first nights gave the author little but sinister suggestions and grotesque food for his imagination. But familiarity dispersed the gloom and the superstitious fancies.

"In the course of a few evenings a thorough

change took place in the scene and its associations. The moon, which when I took possession of my new apartments was invisible, gradually gained each evening upon the darkness of the night, and at length rolled in full splendor above the towers, pouring a flood of tempered light into every court and hall. The garden beneath my window, before wrapped in gloom, was gently lighted up; the orange and citron trees were tipped with silver; the fountain sparkled in the moonbeams, and even the blush of the rose was faintly visible.

"I now felt the poetic merit of the Arabic inscription on the walls,: 'How beauteous is this garden; where the flowers of the earth vie with the stars of heaven. What can compare with the vase of yon alabaster fountain filled with crystal water? nothing but the moon in her fullness, shining in the midst of an unclouded sky!'

"On such heavenly nights I would sit for hours at my window inhaling the sweetness of the garden, and musing on the checkered fortunes of those whose history was dimly shadowed out in the elegant memorials around. Sometimes, when all was quiet, and the clock from the distant cathedral of Granada struck the midnight hour, I have sallied out on another tour and wandered over the whole building; but how different from my first tour! No longer dark and mysterious; no longer peopled with shadowy foes; no longer recalling scenes of violence and murder; all was open, spacious, beautiful; everything called up pleasing and romantic fancies; Lindaraxa once more walked in her garden; the gay chivalry of Moslem Granada once more glittered about the Court of Lions! Who can do justice to a moonlight night in such a climate and such a place? The temperature of a summer midnight in Andalusia is perfectly ethereal. We seem lifted up into a purer atmosphere; we feel a serenity of soul, a buoyancy of spirits, an elasticity of frame, which render mere existence happiness. But when moonlight is added to all this, the effect is like enchantment. Under its plastic sway the Alhambra seems to regain its pristine glories. Every rent and chasm of time, every mouldering tint and weather-stain, is gone; the marble resumes its original whiteness; the long colonnades brighten in the moonbeams; the halls are illuminated with a softened radiance, — we tread the enchanted palace of an Arabian tale!

"What a delight, at such a time, to ascend to the little airy pavilion of the queen's toilet (el tocador de la reyna), which, like a bird-cage, overhangs the valley of the Darro, and gaze from its light arcades upon the moonlight prospect! To the right, the swelling mountains of the

Sierra Nevada, robbed of their ruggedness and softened into a fairy land, with their snowy summits gleaming like silver clouds against the deep blue sky. And then to lean over the parapet of the Tocador and gaze down upon Granada and the Albaycin spread out like a map below; all buried in deep repose; the white palaces and convents sleeping in the moonshine, and beyond all these the vapory vega fading away like a dreamland in the distance.

" Sometimes the faint click of castanets rise from the Alameda, where some gay Andalusians are dancing away the summer night. Sometimes the dubious tones of a guitar and the notes of an amorous voice, tell perchance the whereabout of some moonstruck lover serenading his lady's window.

" Such is a faint picture of the moonlight nights I have passed loitering about the courts and halls and balconies of this most suggestive pile; ' feeding my fancy with sugared suppositions,' and enjoying that mixture of reverie and sensation which steal away existence in a southern climate; so that it has been almost morning before I have retired to bed, and been lulled to sleep by the falling waters of the fountain of Lindaraxa."

One of the writer's vantage points of observation was a balcony of the central win-

dow of the Hall of Ambassadors, from
which he had a magnificent prospect of
mountain, valley, and vega, and could look
down upon a busy scene of human life in
an alameda, or public walk, at the foot of
the hill, and the suburb of the city, filling
the narrow gorge below. Here the author
used to sit for hours, weaving histories out
of the casual incidents passing under his
eye, and the occupations of the busy mortals below. The following passage exhibits
his power in transmuting the commonplace
life of the present into material perfectly in
keeping with the romantic associations of
the place : —

"There was scarce a pretty face or a striking
figure that I daily saw, about which I had not
thus gradually framed a dramatic story, though
some of my characters would occasionally act in
direct opposition to the part assigned them, and
disconcert the whole drama. Reconnoitring one
day with my glass the streets of the Albaycin, I
beheld the procession of a novice about to take
the veil ; and remarked several circumstances
which excited the strongest sympathy in the fate
of the youthful being thus about to be consigned
to a living tomb. I ascertained to my satisfaction

that she was beautiful, and, from the paleness of her cheek, that she was a victim rather than a votary. She was arrayed in bridal garments, and decked with a chaplet of white flowers, but her heart evidently revolted at this mockery of a spiritual union, and yearned after its earthly loves. A tall stern-looking man walked near her in the procession: it was, of course, the tyrannical father, who, from some bigoted or sordid motive, had compelled this sacrifice. Amid the crowd was a dark handsome youth, in Andalusian garb, who seemed to fix on her an eye of agony. It was doubtless the secret lover from whom she was forever to be separated. My indignation rose as I noted the malignant expression painted on the countenances of the attendant monks and friars. The procession arrived at the chapel of the convent; the sun gleamed for the last time upon the chaplet of the poor novice, as she crossed the fatal threshold and disappeared within the building. The throng poured in with cowl, and cross, and minstrelsy; the lover paused for a moment at the door. I could divine the tumult of his feelings; but he mastered them, and entered. There was a long interval. I pictured to myself the scene passing within: the poor novice despoiled of her transient finery, and clothed in the conventual garb; the bridal chaplet taken from her brow, and her beautiful head shorn of

17

its long silken tresses. I heard her murmur the irrevocable vow. I saw her extended on a bier; the death-pall spread over her; the funeral service performed that proclaimed her dead to the world; her sighs were drowned in the deep tones of the organ, and the plaintive requiem of the nuns; the father looked on, unmoved, without a tear; the lover — no — my imagination refused to portray the anguish of the lover — there the picture remained a blank.

" After a time the throng again poured forth and dispersed various ways, to enjoy the light of the sun and mingle with the stirring scenes of life; but the victim, with her bridal chaplet, was no longer there. The door of the convent closed that severed her from the world forever. I saw the father and the lover issue forth; they were in earnest conversation. The latter was vehement in his gesticulations; I expected some violent termination to my drama; but an angle of a building interfered and closed the scene. My eye afterwards was frequently turned to that convent with painful interest. I remarked late at night a solitary light twinkling from a remote lattice of one of its towers. ' There,' said I, ' the unhappy nun sits weeping in her cell, while perhaps her lover paces the street below in unavailing anguish.'

" — The officious Mateo interrupted my meditations and destroyed in an instant the cobweb tissue of my fancy. With his usual zeal he had gathered facts concerning the scene, which put my fictions all to flight. The heroine of my romance was neither young nor handsome; she had no lover; she had entered the convent of her own free will, as a respectable asylum, and was one of the most cheerful residents within its walls.

"It was some little while before I could forgive the wrong done me by the nun in being thus happy in her cell, in contradiction to all the rules of romance; I diverted my spleen, however, by watching, for a day or two, the pretty coquetries of a dark-eyed brunette, who, from the covert of a balcony shrouded with flowering shrubs and a silken awning, was carrying on a mysterious correspondence with a handsome, dark, well-whiskered cavalier, who lurked frequently in the street beneath her window. Sometimes I saw him at an early hour, stealing forth wrapped to the eyes in a mantle. Sometimes he loitered at a corner, in various disguises, apparently waiting for a private signal to slip into the house. Then there was the tinkling of a guitar at night, and a lantern shifted from place to place in the balcony. I imagined another intrigue like that of Almaviva, but was again disconcerted in all my suppositions. The supposed lover turned out to be the husband of the lady, and a noted contra-bandista; and all his mysterious signs and move-ments had doubtless some smuggling scheme in view

" — I occasionally amused myself with noting from this balcony the gradual changes of the scenes below, according to the different stages of the day.

" Scarce has the gray dawn streaked the sky, and the earliest cock crowed from the cottages of the hill-side, when the suburbs give sign of re-viving animation ; for the fresh hours of dawn-ing are precious in the summer season in a sultry climate. All are anxious to get the start of the sun, in the business of the day. The muleteer drives forth his loaded train for the journey ; the traveler slings his carbine behind his saddle, and mounts his steed at the gate of the hostel ; the brown peasant from the country urges for-ward his loitering beasts, laden with panniers of sunny fruit and fresh dewy vegetables, for already the thrifty housewives are hastening to the market.

" The sun is up and sparkles along the valley, tipping the transparent foliage of the groves. The matin bells resound melodiously through the pure bright air, announcing the hour of devotion. The muleteer halts his burdened animals before the chapel, thrusts his staff through his belt be-

hind, and enters with hat in hand, smoothing his
coal-black hair, to hear a mass, and to put up a
prayer for a prosperous wayfaring across the
sierra. And now steals forth on fairy foot the
gentle Señora, in trim basquiña, with restless fan
in hand, and dark eye flashing from beneath the
gracefully folded mantilla; she seeks some well-
frequented church to offer up her morning orisons;
but the nicely adjusted dress, the dainty shoe
and cobweb stocking, the raven tresses exquisitely
braided, the fresh-plucked rose, gleaming among
them like a gem, show that earth divides with
Heaven the empire of her thoughts. Keep an
eye upon her, careful mother, or virgin aunt, or
vigilant duenna, whichever you may be, that
walk behind!

"As the morning advances, the din of labor aug-
ments on every side; the streets are thronged
with man, and steed, and beast of burden, and
there is a hum and murmur, like the surges of
the ocean. As the sun ascends to his meridian,
the hum and bustle gradually decline; at the
height of noon there is a pause. The panting
city sinks into lassitude, and for several hours
there is a general repose. The windows are
closed, the curtains drawn, the inhabtants retired
into the coolest recesses of their mansions; the
full-fed monk snores in his dormitory; the brawny
porter lies stretched on the pavement beside his

burden; the peasant and the laborer sleep beneath the trees of the Alameda, lulled by the sultry chirping of the locust. The streets are deserted, except by the water-carrier, who refreshes the ear by proclaiming the merits of his sparkling beverage, 'colder than the mountain snow (*mas fria que la nieve*).'

"As the sun declines, there is again a gradual reviving, and when the vesper bell rings out his sinking knell, all nature seems to rejoice that the tyrant of the day has fallen. Now begins the bustle of enjoyment, when the citizens pour forth to breathe the evening air, and revel away the brief twilight in the walks and gardens of the Darro and Xenil.

"As night closes, the capricious scene assumes new features. Light after light gradually twinkles forth; here a taper from a balconied window; there a votive lamp before the image of a saint. Thus, by degrees, the city emerges from the pervading gloom, and sparkles with scattered lights, like the starry firmament. Now break forth from court and garden, and street and lane, the tinkling of innumerable guitars, and the clicking of castanets; blending, at this lofty height, in a faint but general concert. 'Enjoy the moment' is the creed of the gay and amorous Andalusian, and at no time does he practice it more zealously than on the balmy nights of summer, wooing his mistress with the dance, the love-ditty, and the passionate serenade."

How perfectly is the illusion of departed splendor maintained in the opening of the chapter on " The Court of Lions."

" The peculiar charm of this old dreamy palace is its power of calling up vague reveries and picturings of the past, and thus clothing naked realities with the illusions of the memory and the imagination. As I delight to walk in these ' vain shadows,' I am prone to seek those parts of the Alhambra which are most favorable to this phantasmagoria of the mind; and none are more so than the Court of Lions, and its surrounding halls. Here the hand of time has fallen the lightest, and the traces of Moorish elegance and splendor exist in almost their original brilliancy. Earthquakes have shaken the foundations of this pile, and rent its rudest towers; yet see! not one of those slender columns has been displaced, not an arch of that light and fragile colonnade given way, and all the fairy fretwork of these domes, apparently as unsubstantial as the crystal fabrics of a morning's frost, exist after the lapse of centuries, almost as fresh as if from the hand of the Moslem artist. I write in the midst of these mementos of the past, in the fresh hour of early morning, in the fated

Hall of the Abencerrages. The blood-stained fountain, the legendary monument of their massacre, is before me; the lofty jet almost casts its dew upon my paper. How difficult to reconcile the ancient tale of violence and blood with the gentle and peaceful scene around! Everything here appears calculated to inspire kind and happy feelings, for everything is delicate and beautiful. The very light falls tenderly from above, through the lantern of a dome tinted and wrought as if by fairy hands. Through the ample and fretted arch of the portal I behold the Court of Lions, with brilliant sunshine gleaming along its colonnades and sparkling in its fountains. The lively swallow dives into the court, and, rising with a surge, darts away twittering over the roofs; the busy bee toils humming among the flower-beds; and painted butterflies hover from plant to plant, and flutter up and sport with each other in the sunny air. It needs but a slight exertion of the fancy to picture some pensive beauty of the harem loitering in these secluded haunts of Oriental luxury.

" He, however, who would behold this scene under an aspect more in unison with its fortunes, let him come when the shadows of evening temper the brightness of the court, and throw a gloom into the surrounding halls. Then nothing can be more serenely melancholy, or more in harmony with the tale of departed grandeur.

" At such times I am apt to seek the Hall of
Justice, whose deep shadowy arcades extend across
the upper end of the court. Here was performed, in presence of Ferdinand and Isabella and
their triumphant court, the pompous ceremonial
of high mass, on taking possession of the Alhambra. The very cross is still to be seen upon the
wall, where the altar was erected, and where
officiated the Grand Cardinal of Spain, and others
of the highest religious dignitaries of the land.
I picture to myself the scene when this place was
filled with the conquering host, that mixture of
mitred prelate and shaven monk, and steel-clad
knight and silken courtier; when crosses and
crosiers and religious standards were mingled
with proud armorial ensigns and the banners of
the haughty chiefs of Spain, and flaunted in triumph through these Moslem halls. I picture to
myself Columbus, the future discoverer of a
world, taking his modest stand in a remote corner, the humble and neglected spectator of the
pageant. I see in imagination the Catholic sovereigns prostrating themselves before the altar,
and pouring forth thanks for their victory; while
the vaults resound with sacred minstrelsy and the
deep-toned Te Deum.

" The transient illusion is over, — the pageant
melts from the fancy, — monarch, priest, and
warrior return into oblivion with the poor Mos-

lems over whom they exulted. The hall of their triumph is waste and desolate. The bat flits about its twilight vault, and the owl hoots from the neighboring tower of Comares."

It is a Moslem tradition that the court and army of Boabdil, the Unfortunate, the last Moorish King of Granada, are shut up in the mountain by a powerful enchantment, and that it is written in the book of fate that when the enchantment is broken, Boabdil will descend from the mountain at the head of his army, resume his throne in the Alhambra, and gathering together the enchanted warriors from all parts of Spain, reconquer the Peninsula. Nothing in this volume is more amusing and at the same time more poetic and romantic than the story of "Governor Manco and the Soldier," in which this legend is used to cover the exploit of a dare-devil contrabandista. But it is too long to quote. I take, therefore, another story, which has something of the same elements, that of a merry, mendicant student of Salamanca, Don Vicente by name, who wandered from village to village, and picked up a living by playing the guitar for the peasants, among whom he was sure of a hearty welcome. In the course of his wandering he had found a seal-ring, having for its device the cabalistic sign, invented by King Solomon the Wise, and of mighty power in all cases of enchantment.

" At length he arrived at the great object of his musical vagabondizing, the far-famed city of Granada, and hailed with wonder and delight its Moorish towers, its lovely vega, and its snowy mountains glistening through a summer atmosphere. It is needless to say with what eager curiosity he entered its gates and wandered through its streets, and gazed upon its Oriental monuments. Every female face peering through a window or beaming from a balcony was to him a Zorayda or a Zelinda, nor could he meet a stately dame on the Alameda but he was ready to fancy her a Moorish princess, and to spread his student's robe beneath her feet.

" His musical talent, his happy humor, his youth and his good looks, won him a universal welcome in spite of his ragged robes, and for several days he led a gay life in the old Moorish capital and its environs. One of his occasional haunts was the fountain of Avellanos, in the valley of Darro. It is one of the popular resorts of Granada, and has been so since the days of the Moors; and here the student had an opportunity of pursuing

his studies of female beauty; a branch of study
to which he was a little prone.

"Here he would take his seat with his guitar,
improvise love-ditties to admiring groups of ma-
jos and majas, or prompt with his music the ever-
ready dance. He was thus engaged one evening
when he beheld a padre of the church advancing,
at whose approach every one touched the hat.
He was evidently a man of consequence; he certainly was a mirror of good if not of holy living; robust and rosy-faced, and breathing at
every pore with the warmth of the weather and
the exercise of the walk. As he passed along
he would every now and then draw a maravedi
out of his pocket and bestow it on a beggar, with
an air of signal beneficence. 'Ah, the blessed
father!' would be the cry; 'long life to him,
and may he soon be a bishop!'

"To aid his steps in ascending the hill he leaned
gently now and then on the arm of a handmaid,
evidently the pet-lamb of this kindest of pastors.
Ah, such a damsel! Andalus from head to foot;
from the rose in her hair, to the fairy shoe and
lacework stocking; Andalus in every movement;
in every undulation of the body: — ripe, melting Andalus!   But then so modest! — so shy!
— ever, with downcast eyes, listening to the
words of the padre; or, if by chance she let
flash a side glance, it was suddenly checked and
her eyes once more cast to the ground.

"The good padre looked benignantly on the company about the fountain, and took his seat with some emphasis on a stone bench, while the handmaid hastened to bring him a glass of sparkling water. He sipped it deliberately and with a relish, tempering it with one of those spongy pieces of frosted eggs and sugar so dear to Spanish epicures, and on returning the glass to the hand of the damsel pinched her cheek with infinite loving-kindness.

"'Ah, the good pastor!' whispered the student to himself; 'what a happiness would it be to be gathered into his fold with such a pet-lamb for a companion!'

"But no such good fare was likely to befall him. In vain he essayed those powers of pleasing which he had found so irresistible with country curates and country lasses. Never had he touched his guitar with such skill; never had he poured forth more soul-moving ditties, but he had no longer a country curate or country lass to deal with. The worthy priest evidently did not relish music, and the modest damsel never raised her eyes from the ground. They remained but a short time at the fountain; the good padre hastened their return to Granada. The damsel gave the student one shy glance in retiring; but it plucked the heart out of his bosom!

"He inquired about them after they had gone.

Padre Tomás was one of the saints of Granada, a model of regularity; punctual in his hour of rising; his hour of taking a paseo for an appe‐ tite; his hours of eating; his hour of taking his siesta; his hour of playing his game of tresillo, of an evening, with some of the dames of the cathedral circle; his hour of supping, and his hour of retiring to rest, to gather fresh strength for another day's round of similar duties. He had an easy sleek mule for his riding; a matronly housekeeper skilled in preparing tidbits for his table; and the pet-lamb, to smooth his pillow at night and bring him his chocolate in the morn‐ ing.

"Adieu now to the gay, thoughtless life of the student; the side-glance of a bright eye had been the undoing of him. Day and night he could not get the image of this most modest damsel out of his mind. He sought the mansion of the pa‐ dre. Alas! it was above the class of houses ac‐ cessible to a strolling student like himself. The worthy padre had no sympathy with him; he had never been *Estudiante sopista*, obliged to sing for his supper. He blockaded the house by day, catching a glance of the damsel now and then as she appeared at a casement; but these glances only fed his flame without encouraging his hope. He serenaded her balcony at night, and at one time was flattered by the appearance of something white at a window. Alas, it was only the night-cap of the padre.

"Never was lover more devoted; never damsel more shy : the poor student was reduced to despair. At length arrived the eve of St. John, when the lower classes of Granada swarm into the country, dance away the afternoon, and pass midsummer's night on the banks of the Darro and the Xenil. Happy are they who on this eventful night can wash their faces in those waters just as the cathedral bell tells midnight ; for at that precise moment they have a beautifying power. The student, having nothing to do, suffered himself to be carried away by the holiday-seeking throng until he found himself in the narrow valley of the Darro, below the lofty hill and ruddy towers of the Alhambra. The dry bed of the river ; the rocks which border it ; the terraced gardens which overhang it, were alive with variegated groups, dancing under the vines and fig-trees to the sound of the guitar and castanets.

"The student remained for some time in doleful dumps, leaning against one of the huge misshapen stone pomegranates which adorn the ends of the little bridge over the Darro. He cast a wistful glance upon the merry scene, where every cavalier had his dame ; or, to speak more appropriately, every Jack his Jill ; sighed at his

own solitary state, a victim to the black eye of
the most unapproachable of damsels, and repined
at his ragged garb, which seemed to shut the gate
of hope against him.

"By degrees his attention was attracted to
a neighbor equally solitary with himself. This
was a tall soldier, of a stern aspect and grizzled
beard, who seemed posted as a sentry at the opposite pomegranate. His face was bronzed by
time; he was arrayed in ancient Spanish armor,
with buckler and lance, and stood immovable as
a statue. What surprised the student was, that
though thus strangely equipped, he was totally
unnoticed by the passing throng, albeit that many
almost brushed against him.

"'This is a city of old time peculiarities,'
thought the student, 'and doubtless this is one
of them with which the inhabitants are too familiar to be surprised.' His own curiosity, however, was awakened, and being of a social disposition, he accosted the soldier.

"'A rare old suit of armor that which you
wear, comrade. May I ask what corps you belong to?'

"The soldier gasped out a reply from a pair of
jaws which seemed to have rusted on their
hinges.

"'The royal guard of Ferdinand and Isabella.'

"'Santa Maria! Why, it is three centuries
since that corps was in service.'

" ' And for three centuries have I been mounting guard. Now I trust my tour of duty draws to a close. Dost thou desire fortune ? '

" The student held up his tattered cloak in reply.

" ' I understand thee. If thou hast faith and courage, follow me, and thy fortune is made.'

" ' Softly, comrade, to follow thee would require small courage in one who has nothing to lose but life and an old guitar, neither of much value ; but my faith is of a different matter, and not to be put in temptation. If it be any criminal act by which I am to mend my fortune, think not my ragged cloak will make me undertake it.'

" The soldier turned on him a look of high displeasure. ' My sword,' said he, ' has never been drawn but in the cause of the faith and the throne. I am a *Cristiano viejo ;* trust in me and fear no evil.'

" The student followed him wondering. He observed that no one heeded their conversation, and that the soldier made his way through the various groups of idlers unnoticed, as if invisible.

" Crossing the bridge, the soldier led the way by a narrow and steep path past a Moorish mill and aqueduct, and up the ravine which separates the domains of the Generalife from those of the Alhambra. The last ray of the sun shone upon the red battlements of the latter, which beetled

18

far above; and the convent-bells were proclaiming the festival of the ensuing day. The ravine
was overshadowed by fig-trees, vines, and myr-
tles, and the outer towers and walls of the fortress. It was dark and lonely, and the twilight-
loving bats began to flit about. At length the
soldier halted at a remote and ruined tower apparently intended to guard a Moorish aqueduct.
He struck the foundation with the butt-end of his
spear. A rumbling sound was heard, and the
solid stones yawned apart, leaving an opening as
wide as a door.

"'Enter in the name of the Holy Trinity,'
said the soldier, 'and fear nothing.' The student's heart quaked, but he made the sign of the
cross, muttered his Ave Maria, and followed his
mysterious guide into a deep vault cut out of the
solid rock under the tower, and covered with Arabic inscriptions. The soldier pointed to a stone
seat hewn along one side of the vault. 'Behold,' said he, 'my couch for three hundred
years.' The bewildered student tried to force a
joke. 'By the blessed St. Anthony,' said he,
'but you must have slept soundly, considering
the hardness of your couch.'

"'On the contrary, sleep has been a stranger to
these eyes; incessant watchfulness has been my
doom. Listen to my lot. I was one of the
royal guards of Ferdinand and Isabella; but

was taken prisoner by the Moors in one of their sorties, and confined a captive in this tower. When preparations were made to surrender the fortress to the Christian sovereigns, I was prevailed upon by an alfaqui, a Moorish priest, to aid him in secreting some of the treasures of Boabdil in this vault. I was justly punished for my fault. The alfaqui was an African necromancer, and by his infernal arts cast a spell upon me — to guard his treasures. Something must have happened to him, for he never returned, and here have I remained ever since, buried alive. Years and years have rolled away; earthquakes have shaken this hill; I have heard stone by stone of the tower above tumbling to the ground, in the natural operation of time; but the spell-bound walls of this vault set both time and earthquakes at defiance.

"'Once every hundred years, on the festival of St. John, the enchantment ceases to have thorough sway; I am permitted to go forth and post myself upon the bridge of the Darro, where you met me, waiting until some one shall arrive who may have power to break this magic spell. I have hitherto mounted guard there in vain. I walk as in a cloud, concealed from mortal sight. You are the first to accost me for now three hundred years. I behold the reason. I see on your finger the seal-ring of Solomon the Wise,

which is proof against all enchantment. With
you it remains to deliver me from this awful
dungeon, or to leave me to keep guard here for
another hundred years.'

"The student listened to this tale in mute won-
derment. He had heard many tales of treasures
shut up under strong enchantment in the vaults
of the Alhambra, but had treated them as fables.
He now felt the value of the seal-ring, which
had, in a manner, been given to him by St. Cy-
prian. Still, though armed by so potent a talis-
man, it was an awful thing to find himself *tête-à-
tête* in such a place with an enchanted soldier,
who, according to the laws of nature, ought to
have been quietly in his grave for nearly three
centuries.

"A personage of this kind, however, was quite
out of the ordinary run, and not to be trifled
with, and he assured him he might rely upon his
friendship and good will to do everything in his
power for his deliverance.

"'I trust to a motive more powerful than
friendship,' said the soldier.

"He pointed to a ponderous iron coffer, secured
by locks inscribed with Arabic characters. 'That
coffer,' said he, 'contains countless treasure in
gold and jewels and precious stones. Break the
magic spell by which I am enthralled, and one
half of this treasure shall be thine.'

" ' But how am I to do it ? '

" 'The aid of a Christian priest and a Christian maid is necessary. The priest to exorcise the powers of darkness; the damsel to touch this chest with the seal of Solomon. This must be done at night. But have a care. This is solemn work, and not to be effected by the carnal-minded. The priest must be a *Cristiano viejo*, a model of sanctity; and must mortify the flesh before he comes here, by a rigorous fast of four-and-twenty hours : and as to the maiden, she must be above reproach, and proof against temptation. Linger not in finding such aid. In three days my furlough is at an end; if not delivered before midnight of the third, I shall have to mount guard for another century.'

" ' Fear not,' said the student, ' I have in my eye the very priest and damsel you describe ; but how am I to regain admission to this tower ? '

" ' The seal of Solomon will open the way for thee.'

" The student issued forth from the tower much more gayly than he had entered. The wall closed behind him, and remained solid as before.

" The next morning he repaired boldly to the mansion of the priest, no longer a poor strolling student, thrumming his way with a guitar; but an ambassador from the shadowy world, with enchanted treasures to bestow. No particulars are told of his negotiation, excepting that the zeal of the worthy priest was easily kindled at the idea of rescuing an old soldier of the faith and a strong box of King Chico from the very clutches of Satan ; and then what alms might be dispensed, what churches built, and how many poor relatives enriched with the Moorish treasure !

"As to the immaculate handmaid, she was ready to lend her hand, which was all that was required, to the pious work ; and if a shy glance now and then might be believed, the ambassador began to find favor in her modest eyes.

"The greatest difficulty, however, was the fast to which the good padre had to subject himself. Twice he attempted it, and twice the flesh was too strong for the spirit. It was only on the third day that he was enabled to withstand the temptations of the cupboard ; but it was still a question whether he would hold out until the spell was broken.

"At a late hour of the night the party groped their way up the ravine by the light of a lantern, and bearing a basket with provisions for exorcising the demon of hunger so soon as the other demons should be laid in the Red Sea.

"The seal of Solomon opened their way into the tower. They found the soldier seated on the enchanted strong-box, awaiting their arrival. The

exorcism was performed in due style. The damsel advanced and touched the locks of the coffer
with the seal of Solomon. The lid flew open;
and such treasures of gold and jewels and precious stones as flashed upon the eye !

"' Here 's cut and come again !' cried the student, exultingly, as he proceeded to cram his
pockets.

"' Fairly and softly,' exclaimed the soldier.
' Let us get the coffer out entire, and then di-
vide.'

" They accordingly went to work with might
and main ; but it was a difficult task ; the chest
was enormously heavy, and had been imbedded
there for centuries. While they were thus employed the good dominie drew on one side and
made a vigorous onslaught on the basket, by way
of exorcising the demon of hunger which was rag-
ing in his entrails. In a little while a fat capon
was devoured, and washed down by a deep pota-
tion of Val de peñas; and, by way of grace after
meat, he gave a kind-hearted kiss to the pet-lamb
who waited on him. It was quietly done in a
corner, but the tell-tale walls babbled it forth as if
in triumph. Never was chaste salute more awful
in its effects. At the sound the soldier gave a
great cry of despair; the coffer, which was half
raised, fell back in its place and was locked once
more. Priest, student, and damsel found them-

selves outside of the tower, the wall of which closed with a thundering jar. Alas! the good padre had broken his fast too soon!

" When recovered from his surprise, the student would have reëntered the tower, but learnt to his dismay that the damsel, in her fright, had let fall the seal of Solomon ; it remained within the vault.

" In a word, the cathedral bell tolled midnight ; the spell was renewed ; the soldier was doomed to mount guard for another hundred years, and there he and the treasure remain to this day — and all because the kind-hearted padre kissed his handmaid. ' Ah, father! father!' said the student, shaking his head ruefully, as they returned down the ravine, ' I fear there was less of the saint than the sinner in that kiss !'

" Thus ends the legend as far as it has been authenticated. There is a tradition, however, that the student had brought off treasure enough in his pocket to set him up in the world ; that he prospered in his affairs, that the worthy padre gave him the pet-lamb in marriage, by way of amends for the blunder in the vault ; that the immaculate damsel proved a pattern for wives as she had been for handmaids, and bore her husband a numerous progeny ; that the first was a wonder ; it was born seven months after her marriage, and though a seven-months' boy, was the sturdiest of the flock. The rest were all born in the ordinary course of time.

"The story of the enchanted soldier remains one of the popular traditions of Granada, though told in a variety of ways; the common people affirm that he still mounts guard on mid-summer eve, beside the gigantic stone pomegranate on the bridge of the Darro; but remains invisible excepting to such lucky mortal as may possess the seal of Solomon."

These passages from the most characteristic of Irving's books, do not by any means exhaust his variety, but they afford a fair measure of his purely literary skill, upon which his reputation must rest. To my apprehension this "charm" in literature is as necessary to the amelioration and enjoyment of human life as the more solid achievements of scholarship. That Irving should find it in the prosaic and materialistic conditions of the New World as well as in the tradition-laden atmosphere of the Old, is evidence that he possessed genius of a refined and subtle quality if not of the most robust order.

CHAPTER X.

LAST YEARS: THE CHARACTER OF HIS LITERATURE.

THE last years of Irving's life, although full of activity and enjoyment, — abated only by the malady which had so long tormented him, — offer little new in the development of his character, and need not much longer detain us. The calls of friendship and of honor were many, his correspondence was large, he made many excursions to scenes that were filled with pleasant memories, going even as far south as Virginia, and he labored assiduously at the "Life of Washington," — attracted however now and then by some other tempting theme. But his delight was in the domestic circle at Sunnyside. It was not possible that his occasional melancholy vein should not be deepened by change and death and the lengthening shade of old age. Yet I do not know the closing days of any

other author of note that were more cheerful, serene, and happy than his. Of our
author, in these latter days, Mr. George
William Curtis put recently into his "Easy
Chair" papers an artistically-touched little
portrait: "Irving was as quaint a figure,"
he says, "as the Diedrich Knickerbocker in
the preliminary advertisement of the 'History of New York.' Thirty years ago he
might have been seen on an autumnal afternoon tripping with an elastic step along
Broadway, with 'low-quartered' shoes neatly
tied, and a Talma cloak — a short garment
that hung from the shoulders like the cape
of a coat. There was a chirping, cheery,
old-school air in his appearance which was
undeniably Dutch, and most harmonious
with the associations of his writing. He
seemed, indeed, to have stepped out of his
own books; and the cordial grace and humor of his address, if he stopped for a passing chat, were delightfully characteristic.
He was then our most famous man of letters, but he was simply free from all self-
consciousness and assumption and dogma-
tism." Congenial occupation was one secret
of Irving's cheerfulness and contentment,

no doubt. And he was called away as soon as his task was done, very soon after the last volume of the " Washington " issued from the press. Yet he lived long enough to receive the hearty approval of it from the literary men whose familiarity with the Revolutionary period made them the best judges of its merits.

He had time also to revise his works. It is perhaps worthy of note that for several years, while he was at the height of his popularity, his books had very little sale. From 1842 to 1848 they were out of print, with the exception of some stray copies of a cheap Philadelphia edition, and a Paris collection (a volume of this, at my hand, is one of a series entitled a " Collection of Ancient and Modern *British* Authors"), they were not to be found. The Philadelphia publishers did not think there was sufficient demand to warrant a new edition. Mr. Irving and his friends judged the market more wisely, and a young New York publisher offered to assume the responsibility. This was Mr. George P. Putnam. The event justified his sagacity and his liberal enterprise ; from July, 1848, to November, 1859, the author received on his copyright over eighty-eight thousand dollars. And it should be added that the relations between author and publisher, both in prosperity and in times of business disaster, reflect the highest credit upon both. If the like relations always obtained we should not have to say : " May the Lord pity the authors in this world, and the publishers in the next."

I have outlined the life of Washington Irving in vain, if we have not already come to a tolerably clear conception of the character of the man and of his books. If I were exactly to follow his literary method I should do nothing more. The idiosyncrasies of the man are the strength and weakness of his works. I do not know any other author whose writings so perfectly reproduce his character, or whose character may be more certainly measured by his writings. His character is perfectly transparent : his predominant traits were humor and sentiment; his temperament was gay with a dash of melancholy ; his inner life and his mental operations were the reverse of complex, and his literary method is simple. He *felt* his subject, and he expressed his conception not so much by direct statement or description as by almost imperceptible touches and shadings here and there, by a diffused tone and color, with very little show of analysis. Perhaps it is a sufficient definition to say that his method was the sympathetic. In the end the reader is put in possession of the luminous and complete idea upon which the author has been brooding, though he may not be able to say exactly how the impression has been conveyed to him; and I doubt if the author could have explained his sympathetic process. He certainly would have lacked precision in any philosophical or metaphysical theme, and when, in his letters, he touches upon politics there is a little vagueness of definition that indicates want of mental grip in that direction. But in the region of feeling his genius is sufficient to his purpose; either when that purpose is a highly creative one, as in the character and achievements of his Dutch heroes, or merely that of portraiture, as in the " Columbus " and the " Washington." The analysis of a nature so simple and a character so transparent as Irving's, who lived in the sunlight and had no envelope of mystery, has not the fascination that attaches to Hawthorne.

Although the direction of his work as a man of letters was largely determined by his early surroundings, — that is, by his birth in a land void of traditions, and into a society without much literary life, so that his intellectual food was of necessity a foreign literature that was at the moment becoming a little antiquated in the land of its birth, and his warm imagination was forced to revert to the past for that nourishment which his crude environment did not offer,— yet he was by nature a retrospective man. His face was set towards the past, not towards the future. He never caught the restlessness of this century, nor the prophetic light that shone in the faces of Coleridge, Shelley, and Keats ; if he apprehended the stir of the new spirit he still, by mental affiliation, belonged rather to the age of Addison than to that of Macaulay. And his placid, retrospective, optimistic strain pleased a public that were excited and harrowed by the mocking and lamenting of

Lord Byron, and, singularly enough, pleased even the great pessimist himself.

His writings induce to reflection, to quiet musing, to tenderness for tradition; they amuse, they entertain, they call a check to the feverishness of modern life; but they are rarely stimulating or suggestive. They are better adapted, it must be owned, to please the many than the critical few, who demand more incisive treatment and a deeper consideration of the problems of life. And it is very fortunate that a writer who can reach the great public and entertain it can also elevate and refine its tastes, set before it high ideas, instruct it agreeably, and all this in a style that belongs to the best literature. It is a safe model for young readers; and for young readers there is very little in the overwhelming flood of to-day that is comparable to Irving's books, and, especially, it seems to me, because they were not written for children.

Irving's position in American literature, or in that of the English tongue, will only be determined by the slow settling of opinion, which no critic can foretell, and the operation of which no criticism seems able to explain. I venture to believe, however, that the verdict will not be in accord with much of the present prevalent criticism. The service that he rendered to American letters no critic disputes; nor is there any question of our national indebtedness to him for investing a crude and new land with the enduring charms of romance and tradition. In this respect, our obligation to him is that of Scotland to Scott and Burns; and it is an obligation due only, in all history, to here and there a fortunate creator to whose genius opportunity is kind. The Knickerbocker Legend and the romance with which Irving has invested the Hudson are a priceless legacy; and this would remain an imperishable possession in popular tradition if the literature creating it were destroyed. This sort of creation is unique in modern times. New York is the Knickerbocker city; its whole social life remains colored by his fiction; and the romantic background it owes to him in some measure supplies to it what great age has given to European cities. This creation is sufficient to secure for him an immortality, a length of earthly remem-

19

brance that all the rest of his writings together might not give.

Irving was always the literary man; he had the habits, the idiosyncrasies, of his small genus. I mean that he regarded life not from the philanthropic, the economic, the political, the philosophic, the metaphysic, the scientific, or the theologic, but purely from the literary point of view. He belongs to that small class of which Johnson and Goldsmith are perhaps as good types as any, and to which America has added very few. The literary point of view is taken by few in any generation; it may seem to the world of very little consequence in the pressure of all the complex interests of life, and it may even seem trivial amid the tremendous energies applied to immediate affairs; but it is the point of view that endures; if its creations do not mould human life, like the Roman law, they remain to charm and civilize, like the poems of Horace You must not ask more of them than that. This attitude toward life is defensible on the highest grounds. A man with Irving's gifts has the right to take the position of an observer and describer, and not to be called on for a more active participation in affairs than he chooses to take. He is doing the world the highest service of which he is capable, and the most enduring it can receive from any man. It is not a question whether the work of the literary man is higher than that of the reformer or the statesman; it is a distinct work, and is justified by the result, even when the work is that of the humorist only. We recognize this in the case of the poet. Although Goethe has been reproached for his lack of sympathy with the liberalizing movement of his day (as if his novels were quieting social influences), it is felt by this generation that the author of "Faust" needs no apology that he did not spend his energies in the effervescing politics of the German states. I mean, that while we may like or dislike the man for his sympathy or want of sympathy, we concede to the author the right of his attitude; if Goethe had not assumed freedom from moral responsibility, I suppose that criticism of his aloofness would long ago have ceased. Irving did not lack sympathy with humanity in the concrete; it colored whatever he wrote.

But he regarded the politics of his own country, the revolutions in France, the long struggle in Spain, without heat; and he held aloof from projects of agitation and reform, and maintained the attitude of an observer, regarding the life about him from the point of view of the literary artist, as he was justified in doing.

Irving had the defects of his peculiar genius, and these have no doubt helped to fix upon him the complimentary disparagement of "genial." He was not aggressive; in his nature he was wholly unpartisan, and full of lenient charity; and I suspect that his kindly regard of the world, although returned with kindly liking, cost him something of that respect for sturdiness and force which men feel for writers who flout them as fools in the main. Like Scott, he belonged to the idealists, and not to the realists, whom our generation affects. Both writers stimulate the longing for something better. Their creed was short: "Love God and honor the King." It is a very good one for a literary man, and might do for a Christian. The supernatural was still a reality in the age in which they wrote.

Irving's faith in God and his love of humanity were very simple; I do not suppose he was much disturbed by the deep problems that have set us all adrift. In every age, whatever is astir, literature, theology, all intellectual activity, takes one and the same drift, and approximates in color. The bent of Irving's spirit was fixed in his youth, and he escaped the desperate realism of this generation, which has no outcome, and is likely to produce little that is noble.

I do not know how to account, on principles of culture which we recognize, for our author's style. His education was exceedingly defective, nor was his want of discipline supplied by subsequent desultory application. He seems to have been born with a rare sense of literary proportion and form; into this, as into a mould, were run his apparently lazy and really acute observations of life. That he thoroughly mastered such literature as he fancied there is abundant evidence; that his style was influenced by the purest English models is also apparent. But there remains a large margin for wonder how, with his want of training, he could have elaborated a style which is distinctively his own, and is as copious, felicitous in the choice of words, flowing, spontaneous, flexible, engaging, clear, and as little wearisome when read continuously in quantity as any in the English tongue. This is saying a great deal, though it is not claiming for him the compactness, nor the robust vigor, nor the depth of thought, of many others masters in it. It is sometimes praised for its simplicity. It is certainly lucid, but its simplicity is not that of Benjamin Franklin's style; it is often ornate, not seldom somewhat diffuse, and always exceedingly melodious. It is noticeable for its metaphorical felicity. But it was not in the sympathetic nature of the author, to which I just referred, to come sharply to the point. It is much to have merited the eulogy of Campbell that he had " added clarity to the English tongue." This elegance and finish of style (which seems to have been as natural to the man as his amiable manner) is sometimes made his reproach, as if it were his sole merit, and as if he had concealed under this charming form a want of substance. In literature form is vital. But his case does not rest upon that. As an illustration his " Life of Washington " may be put in evidence. Probably this work lost something in incisiveness and brilliancy by being postponed till the writer's old age. But whatever this loss, it is impossible for any biography to be less pretentious in style, or less ambitious in proclamation. The only pretension of matter is in the early chapters, in which a more than doubtful genealogy is elaborated, and in which it is thought necessary to Washington's dignity to give a fictitious importance to his family and his childhood, and to accept the southern estimate of the hut in which he was born as a " mansion." In much of this false estimate Irving was doubtless misled by the fables of Weems. But while he has given us a dignified portrait of Washington, it is as far as possible removed from that of the smileless prig which has begun to weary even the popular fancy. The man he paints is flesh and blood, presented, I believe, with substantial faithfulness to his character ; with a recognition of the defects of his education and the deliberation of his mental operations ; with at least a hint of that want of breadth of culture and knowledge of the past, the possession of which characterized many of his great associates; and with no concealment that he had a dower of passions and a temper which only vigorous self-watchfulness kept under. But he portrays, with an admiration not too highly colored, the magnificent patience, the courage to bear misconstruction, the unfailing patriotism, the practical sagacity, the level balance of judgment combined with the wisest toleration, the dignity of mind, and the lofty moral nature which made him the great man of his epoch. Irving's grasp of this character; his lucid marshaling of the scattered, often wearisome and uninteresting details of our dragging, unpicturesque Revolutionary War; his just judgment of men; his even, almost judicial, moderation of tone; and his admirable proportion of space to events, render the discussion of style in reference to this work superfluous. Another writer might have made a more brilliant performance: descriptions sparkling with antitheses, characters projected into startling attitudes by the use of epithets; a work more exciting and more piquant, that would have started a thousand controversies, and engaged the attention by daring conjectures and attempts to make a dramatic spectacle ; a book interesting and notable, but false in philosophy and untrue in fact.

When the " Sketch-Book " appeared, an English critic said it should have been first published in England, for Irving was an English writer. The idea has been more than once echoed here. The truth is that while Irving was intensely American in feeling he was first of all a man of letters, and in that capacity he was cosmopolitan ; he certainly was not insular. He had a rare accommodation of tone to his theme. Of England, whose traditions kindled his susceptible fancy, he wrote as Englishmen would like to write about it. In Spain he was saturated with the romantic story of the people and the fascination of the clime ; and he was so true an interpreter of both as to earn from the Spaniards the title of " the poet Irving." I chanced once, in an inn at Frascati, to take up " The Tales of a Traveller," which I had not seen for many years. I expected to revive the somewhat faded humor and fancy of the past generation. But I found not only a sprightly humor and vivacity which are modern, but a truth to Italian local color that is very rare in any writer foreign to the soil. As to America, I do not know what can be more characteristically American than the Knickerbocker, the Hudson River tales, the sketches of life and adventure in the far West. But underneath all this diversity there is one constant quality, — the flavor of the author. Open by chance and read almost anywhere in his score of books, — it may be the " Tour on the Prairies," the familiar dream of the Alhambra, or the narratives of the brilliant exploits of New World explorers; surrender yourself to the flowing current of his transparent style, and you are conscious of a beguilement which is the crowning excellence of all lighter literature, for which we have no word but " charm."

The consensus of opinion about Irving in England and America for thirty years was very remarkable. He had a universal popularity rarely enjoyed by any writer. England returned him to America medalled by the king, honored by the university which is chary of its favors, followed by the applause of the whole English people. In English households, in drawing-rooms of the metropolis in political circles no less than among the literary coteries, in the best reviews, and in the popular newspapers the opinion of him was pretty much the same. And even in the lapse of time and the change of literary fashion authors so unlike as Byron and Dickens were equally warm in admiration of him. To the English indorsement America added her own enthusiasm, which was as universal. His readers were the million, and all his readers were admirers. Even American statesmen, who feed their minds on food we know not of, read Irving. It is true that the uncritical opinion of New York was never exactly re-echoed in the cool recesses of Boston culture ; but the magnates of the " North American Review " gave him their meed of cordial praise. The country at large put him on a pinnacle. If you attempt to account for the position he occupied by his character, which won the love of all men, it must be remembered that the quality which won this, whatever its value, pervades his books also.

And yet it must be said that the total impression left upon the mind by the man and his works is not that of the greatest intellectual force. I have no doubt that this was the impression he made upon his ablest contemporaries. And this fact, when I consider the effect the man produced, makes the study of him all the more interesting. As an intellectual personality he makes no such impression, for instance, as Carlyle, or a dozen other writers now living who could be named. The incisive critical faculty was almost entirely wanting in him. He had neither the power nor the disposition to cut his way transversely across popular opinion and prejudice that Ruskin has, nor to draw around him disciples equally well pleased to see him fiercely demolish to-day what they had delighted to see him set up yesterday as eternal. He evoked neither violent partisanship nor violent opposition. He was an extremely sensitive man, and if he had been capable of creating a conflict he would only have been miserable in it. The play of his mind depended upon the sunshine of approval. And all this shows a certain want of intellectual virility.

A recent anonymous writer has said that
most of the writing of our day is characterized by an intellectual strain. I have no
doubt that this will appear to be the case
to the next generation. It is a strain to
say something new even at the risk of par-
adox, or to say something in a new way
at the risk of obscurity. From this Irving
was entirely free. There is no visible strain-
ing to attract attention. His mood is calm
and unexaggerated. Even in some of his
pathos, which is open to the suspicion of
being "literary," there is no literary exaggeration. He seems always writing from
an internal calm, which is the necessary
condition of his production. If he wins at
all by his style, by his humor, by his portraiture of scenes or of character, it is by a
gentle force, like that of the sun in spring.
There are many men now living, or recently
dead, intellectual prodigies, who have stim-
ulated thought, upset opinions, created mental eras, to whom Irving stands hardly in
as fair a relation as Goldsmith to Johnson.
What verdict the next generation will put
upon their achievements I do not know;
but it is safe to say that their position and

that of Irving as well will depend largely upon the affirmation or the reversal of their views of life and their judgments of character. I think the calm work of Irving will stand when much of the more startling and perhaps more brilliant intellectual achievement of this age has passed away.

And this leads me to speak of Irving's moral quality, which I cannot bring myself to exclude from a literary estimate, even in the face of the current gospel of art for art's sake. There is something that made Scott and Irving personally loved by the millions of their readers, who had only the dimmest ideas of their personality. This was some quality perceived in what they wrote. Each one can define it for himself; there it is, and I do not see why it is not as integral a part of the authors — an element in the estimate of their future position — as what we term their intellect, their knowledge, their skill, or their art. However you rate it, you cannot account for Irving's influence in the world without it. In his tender tribute to Irving, the great-hearted Thackeray, who saw as clearly as anybody the place of mere literary art in the sum total of life, quoted the dying words of Scott to Lockhart, — " Be a good man, my dear." We know well enough that the great author of " The Newcomes" and the great author of " The Heart of Midlothian " recognized the abiding value in literature of integrity, sincerity, purity, charity, faith. These are beneficences; and Irving's literature, walk round it and measure it by whatever critical instruments you will, is a beneficent literature. The author loved good women and little children and a pure life; he had faith in his fellow-men, a kindly sympathy with the lowest, without any subservience to the highest; he retained a belief in the possibility of chivalrous actions, and did not care to envelop them in a cynical suspicion; he was an author still capable of an enthusiam. His books are wholesome, full of sweetness and charm, of humor without any sting, of amusement without any stain ; and their more solid qualities are marred by neither pedantry nor pretension.

Washington Irving died on the 28th of November, 1859, at the close of a lovely day of that Indian Summer which is nowhere more full of a melancholy charm than on the banks of the lower Hudson, and which was in perfect accord with the ripe and peaceful close of his life. He was buried on a little elevation overlooking Sleepy Hollow and the river he loved, amidst the scenes which his magic pen has made classic and his sepulchre hallows.

CHARLES DUDLEY WARNER (1829-1900), editor of the original American Men of Letters series, studied law in his youth but abandoned the legal profession for a literary career. Longtime editor of the *Hartford Courant*, he also collaborated with Mark Twain on *The Gilded Age* and wrote numerous popular essays, nostalgic sketches, and travel books, among them *My Summer in a Garden, Being a Boy, Backlog Studies, In the Levant,* and *Fashions in Literature.*

PHILIP MCFARLAND is the author of *Sojourners,* an account of the age of Washington Irving. He currently teaches English at Concord Academy in Concord, Massachusetts.